SINGER

SEWING REFERENCE LIBRARY®

Window Treatments

COWLES
Creative Publishing

A Division of Cowles Enthusiast Media, Inc.
Minnetonka, Minnesota, USA

SINGER

SEWING REFERENCE LIBRARY®

Window Treatments

Contents

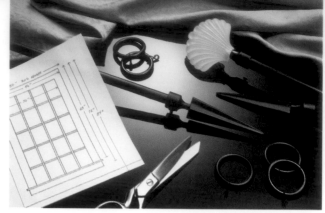

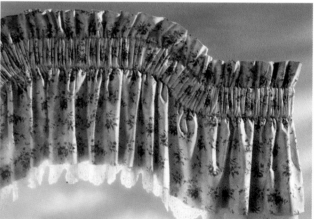

Copyright © 1996
Cowles Creative Publishing, Inc.
Formerly Cy DeCosse Incorporated
5900 Green Oak Drive
Minnetonka, Minnesota 55343
1-800-328-3895
All rights reserved
Printed in U.S.A.

Books available in this series:
Sewing Essentials, Sewing for the Home, Clothing Care & Repair, Sewing for Style, Sewing Specialty Fabrics, Sewing Activewear, The Perfect Fit, Timesaving Sewing, More Sewing for the Home, Tailoring, Sewing for Children, Sewing with an Overlock, 101 Sewing Secrets, Sewing Pants That Fit, Quilting by Machine, Decorative Machine Stitching, Creative Sewing Ideas, Sewing Lingerie, Sewing Projects for the Home,

Sewing with Knits, More Creative Sewing Ideas, Quilt Projects by Machine, Creating Fashion Accessories, Quick & Easy Sewing Projects, Sewing for Special Occasions, Sewing for the Holidays, Quick & Easy Decorating Projects, Quilted Projects & Garments, Embellished Quilted Projects, Window Treatments

Library of Congress
Cataloging-in-Publication Data

Window treatments.
p. cm. — (Singer sewing reference library)
Includes index.
ISBN 0-86573-407-0
ISBN 0-86573-408-9 (pbk.)
1. Drapery. 2. Drapery in interior decoration. I. Cy DeCosse Incorporated. II. Series.
TT390.W55 1996
646.2'1 – dc20   96-41124

COWLES
Creative Publishing
A Division of Cowles Enthusiast Media, Inc.

President/COO: Nino Tarantino
Executive V. P./Editor-in-Chief:
  William B. Jones

WINDOW TREATMENTS

Created by: The Editors of Cowles Creative
Publishing, in cooperation with the
Sewing Education Department, Singer
Sewing Company. Singer is a trademark
of The Singer Company Limited and is
used under license.
Group Executive Editor: Zoe A. Graul
Managing Editor: Elaine Johnson
Project Manager: Amy Friebe
Writer: Linda Neubauer

Associate Creative Director: Lisa Rosenthal
Senior Art Director: Delores Swanson
Editor: Janice Cauley
Sample Production Manager: Carol Olson
Senior Technical Photo Stylist:
    Bridget Haugh
Technical Photo Stylists: Sue Jorgensen,
    Nancy Sundeen
Project & Prop Stylist: Coralie Sathre
Lead Samplemaker: Carol Pilot
Sewing Staff: Arlene Dohrman, Phyllis
    Galbraith, Bridget Haugh, Valerie Hill,
    Kristi Kuhnau, Virginia Mateen,
    Michelle Skudlarek, Nancy Sundeen
V. P. Photography & Production: Jim Bindas
Studio Services Manager: Marcia Chambers
Photo Services Coordinator: Cheryl Neisen
Photo Scheduler: Cathleen Shannon
Lead Photographer: Rex Irmen

Photographer: Chuck Nields
Photography Assistants: Mike Sipe,
    Greg Wallace
Publishing Production Manager: Kim Gerber
Desktop Publishing Specialist:
    Laurie Kristensen
Production Staff: Laura Hokkanen, Tom
    Hoops, Mike Schauer, Kay Wethern
Shop Supervisor: Phil Juntti
Lead Carpenter: Troy Johnson
Carpenter: Rob Johnstone
Contributors: A. Svensson & Company;
    American and Efrid, Inc.; Bandex
    Home Decorating Corporation; Bentley
    Brothers; Conso Products Company; Dritz
    Corporation; Gene Smiley Showroom;
    Graber Industries, Inc./Springs Window
    Fashion Division; Hirshfields Design
    Studio; Kirsch Division, Cooper
    Industries, Inc.; Murtra Industries,
    U.S.A.; Swavelle/Mill Creek Textiles;
    Waverly, Division of F. Schumacher &
    Company

Page references for contributors'
    products are listed on page 127.

Printed on American paper by:
R. R. Donnelley & Sons Co.
99 98 97 96 / 5 4 3 2 1

COWLES
Enthusiast Media

President/COO: Philip L. Penny

Introduction

Roman Shades, page 23.

Window treatments have powerful impact on the decorating plan of a home. Through their style, fabric, and color, they set the mood in every room. Whether you are starting with a new home or rejuvenating your present decorating plan, *Window Treatments* offers you many ideas and expert instructions to create the look you want.

In the Getting Started section, you will find valuable information, basic to every window treatment project. You will learn techniques for accurately measuring the window and determining yardage requirements. There are expert tips for cutting and sewing decorator fabrics, including methods for matching prints and plaids. Detailed instructions help you select and install hardware and make your own mounting boards.

Roman shades offer privacy, light control, and simple style, besides being one of the easiest treatments to sew. In the Roman Shades section, you will find instructions for three shades, each with its own unique look.

Valances, page 43.

The valance is often the focal point of the window treatment. In the Valances section, you will discover a wide selection of top treatment styles, some installed on rods and others mounted on boards. These valances can be used alone or as a finishing touch over many other window treatment styles, from simple blinds and pleated shades to floor-length curtains and draperies.

In the Curtains section, there are several fresh styles, including scalloped curtains, button-tab curtains, and curtains with attached valances or contrasting cuffs. Some curtains are installed on decorator rods, using the newest innovations in decorative hardware. You will learn simple techniques for using self-styling tapes and discover how to create a padded effect with flannel interlining.

Often it is the added flourish that transforms a successful window treatment into a dramatic statement. In the Embellishments section, you will find a variety of ideas and tips for adding detail and personality to your new creation. Use welting in outer seams as a subtle, but effective, accent. Make a bold change simply by banding the edges of a window treatment. Add a touch of elegance with fringe, or get creative with cords and tassels.

Curtains, page 79.

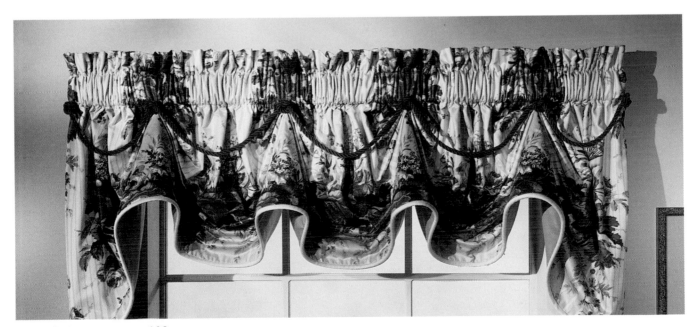

Embellishments, page 109.

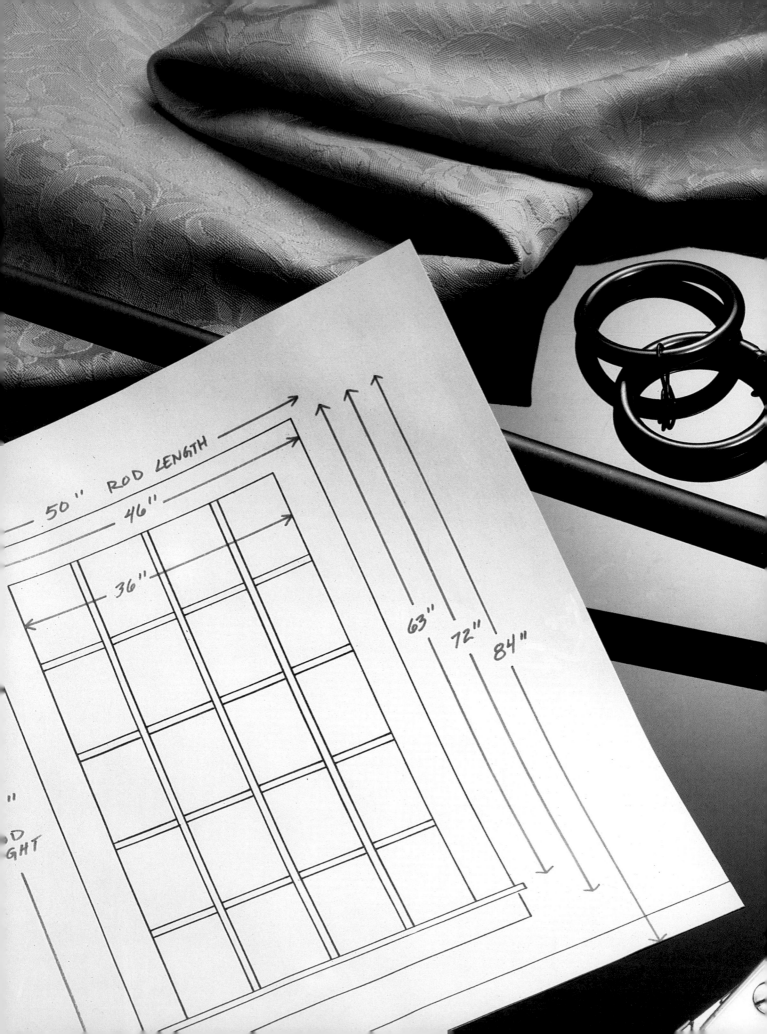

Measuring the Window

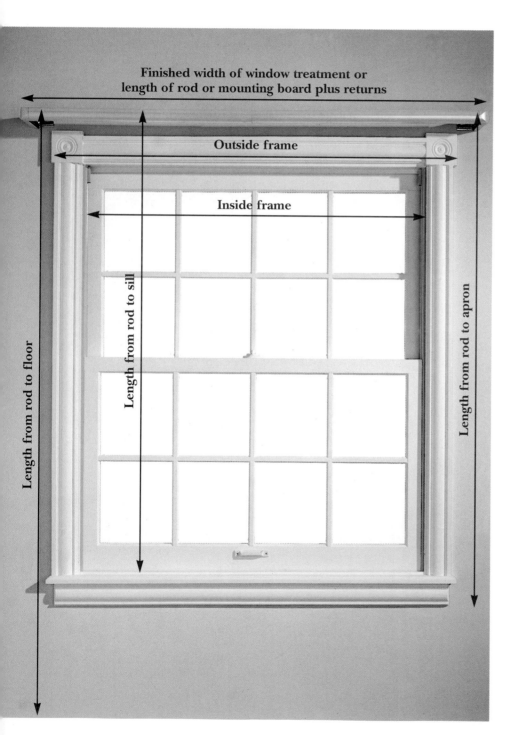

**Finished width of window treatment or
length of rod or mounting board plus returns**

Outside frame

Inside frame

Length from rod to sill

Length from rod to floor

Length from rod to apron

Sketch the window treatment to scale on graph paper, to help you determine the most pleasing proportion for the treatment as well as the correct placement of any hardware. After installing the hardware, take all necessary measurements, using a steel tape measure for accuracy, and record the measurements on the sketch.

For each project, you will need to determine the finished length and width of the treatment. The finished length is measured from the top of the mounting board or rod, or from where you want the upper edge of a curtain, to where you want the lower edge of the window treatment. The finished width is determined by measuring the length of the rod or mounting board. For treatments with returns, the finished width includes twice the projection of the rod or mounting board.

Specific instructions for determining the cut lengths and widths of the fabric are given for each project in this book. In general, the cut width is determined by multiplying the finished width by the amount of fullness desired. Fullness describes the finished width of the curtain or valance in proportion to the length of the rod or mounting board. For example, two times fullness means that the width of the curtain measures two times the length of the rod.

Yardage requirements can be determined by multiplying the cut length by the number of fabric widths needed to obtain the cut width. Special considerations for determining yardage requirements for patterned fabrics are given on page 14.

Tips for Measuring

Plan the proportion of the layers in a window treatment so the length of the top treatment is about one-fifth the length of the overall treatment. The top treatment may be installed higher than the window, to add visual height to the overall treatment. In some cases, it may be desirable to start the top treatment at the ceiling, provided the top of the window frame is not visible at the lower edge of the top treatment.

Plan for the shortest point of a top treatment to fall at least 4" to 6" (10 to 15 cm) below the top of the window glass. This prevents you from seeing the window frame as you look upward at the top treatment.

Allow ½" (1.3 cm) clearance between the lower edge of the curtain and the floor when measuring for floor-length curtains.

Add 2" (5 cm) to the measurement for floor-length curtains for a window treatment that breaks on the floor (page 80).

Add 20" (51 cm) to the measurement for floor-length curtains for a window treatment that puddles on the floor.

Measure for all curtains in the room to the same height from the floor, for a uniform look. Use the highest window in the room as the standard for measuring the other windows.

Terms to Know

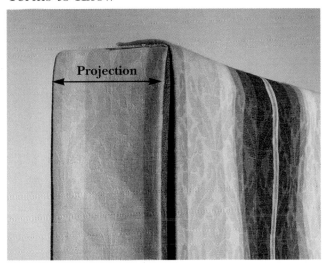

Projection is the distance the rod or mounting board stands out from the wall.

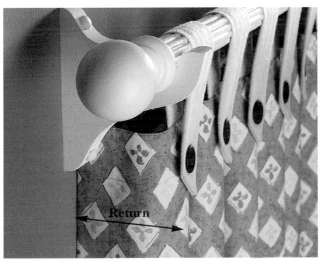

Return is the portion of the curtain or top treatment extending from the end of the rod or mounting board to the wall, blocking the side light and view.

The heading (a) is the portion at the top of a rod-pocket window treatment that forms a ruffle when the curtain is on the rod. The depth of the heading is the distance from the top of the finished curtain to the top stitching line of the rod pocket.

The rod pocket (b) is the portion of the curtain where the curtain rod or pole is inserted. Stitching lines at the top and bottom of the rod pocket keep the rod or pole in place. To determine the depth of the rod pocket, measure around the widest point of the rod or pole; add ½" (1.3 cm) for ease, and divide this amount by two.

Cutting & Sewing Decorator Fabrics

Successful window treatment projects begin with careful preparation, cutting, and seaming of the fabric. Because of the wide variety of decorator fabrics available, there are many options for each of these steps. Characteristics, including fiber content, style and tightness of weave, and any added finishes, should be considered.

Preshrinking is recommended, to ensure that fabrics will not shrink during construction or when first cleaned. Window treatments are only washable if they are made with washable fabric and have no other nonwashable components, such as lining, interlining, interfacings, or trims. Most window treatments are not washable, and should be dry-cleaned when necessary. Fabric, lining, and any other components can be preshrunk, using a steam iron, *before they are cut.*

To ensure that a treatment will hang correctly, fabric lengths must be cut and sewn on grain. Tightly woven fabrics that do not need to be matched at the seams may be cut perpendicular to the selvage, using a carpenter's square as a guide for marking the cutting line. For lightweight and loosely woven fabrics, such as sheers and casements, it is easier and more accurate to pull a thread along the crosswise grain and cut along the pulled thread.

For window treatments with wide, flat expanses, such as mock cornices (page 73), it is desirable to eliminate seams by railroading the fabric. The lengthwise grain of the fabric is run horizontally on the window treatment. This works well for fabrics with solid colors or nondirectional prints, as well as for some plaids.

Types of Seams

Straight-stitch seam, sewn on the conventional sewing machine, is pressed open for a smooth, flat seam. Trim the selvages away either before or after seaming fabric. For lined window treatments, it is not necessary to finish the seam allowances.

Zigzag seam, stitched with a narrow zigzag stitch, is used on lace and loosely woven fabrics to prevent puckering along the seamline. Clip the selvages of loosely woven fabrics every 2" (5 cm), rather than trim them away. Seam allowances may be pressed open or to one side.

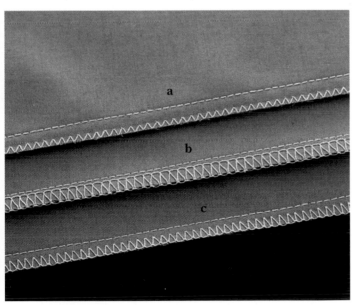

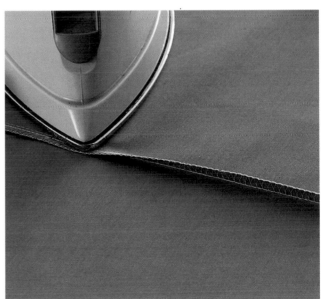

Combination seams are stitched using the straight stitch on the conventional sewing machine. The seam allowances are trimmed to ¼" (6 mm), trimming away the selvages, and finished using a conventional zigzag stitch (**a**), or a 3-thread (**b**) or 2-thread (**c**) overlock stitch on a serger. Press the seam allowances to one side.

4-thread or 5-thread overlock seam, stitched on a serger, is self-finished and does not stretch out of shape. Press the seam allowances to one side.

Working with Patterned Fabrics

Patterned decorator fabrics are designed to be matched at the seams. Cuts are made across the fabric, from selvage to selvage, following the pattern repeat rather than the fabric grain, so it is very important to purchase fabric that has been printed on grain. Fabrics that are printed slightly off grain can usually be corrected by stretching diagonally, unless they have a polished finish.

The pattern repeat is the lengthwise distance from one distinctive point in the pattern, such as the tip of a particular petal in a floral pattern, to the same point in the next pattern design. Some patterned fabrics have pattern repeat markings (+) printed on the selvage. These markings indicate the beginning of each pattern repeat, and they are especially helpful for fabrics that include several similar designs.

Extra yardage is usually needed in order to match the pattern. Add the amounts needed for any hems, rod

pockets, headings, ease, and seam allowances to the finished length, to determine how long the lengths of fabric need to be. Then round this measurement up to the next number divisible by the size of the pattern repeat to determine the cut length. For example, if the pattern repeat (a) is 24" (61 cm), and the needed length (b) is 45" (115 cm), the actual cut length (c) is 48" (122 cm). To have patterns match from one panel to the next, each panel must be cut at exactly the same point of the pattern repeat.

To calculate the amount of fabric needed, multiply the cut length by the number of fabric widths required for the project; add one additional pattern repeat so you can adjust the placement of the pattern on the cut lengths. This is the total fabric length in inches (centimeters); divide this measurement by 36" (100 cm) to determine the number of yards (meters) required.

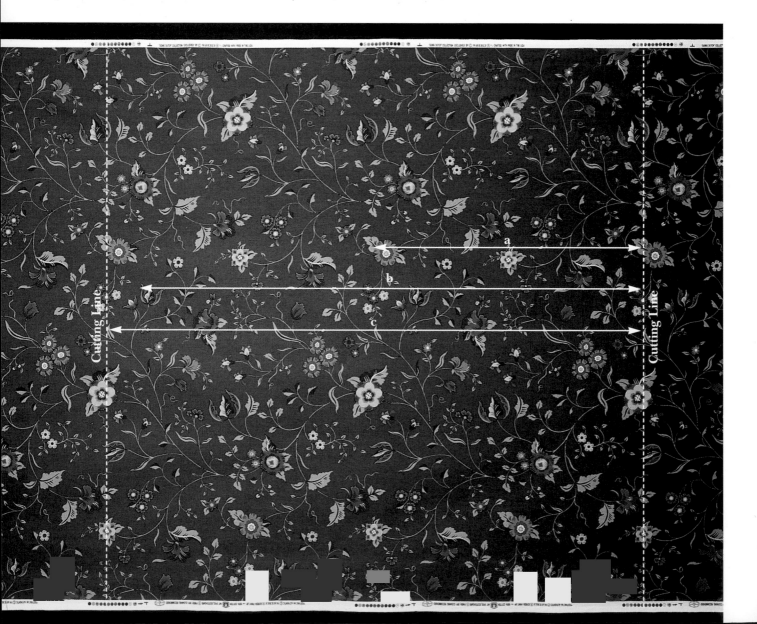

How to Match a Patterned Fabric

1) **Position** the fabric widths right sides together, matching selvages.

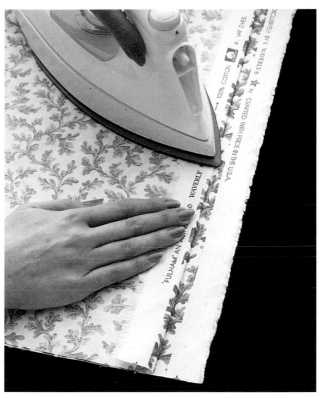

2) **Fold** back upper selvage until the pattern matches; press foldline.

3) **Unfold** selvage, and pin fabric widths together on foldline. Check the match from right side.

4) **Repin** the fabric so pins are perpendicular to the foldline; stitch on foldline. Trim away selvages. Trim the fabric to finished length plus other allowances, as calculated opposite.

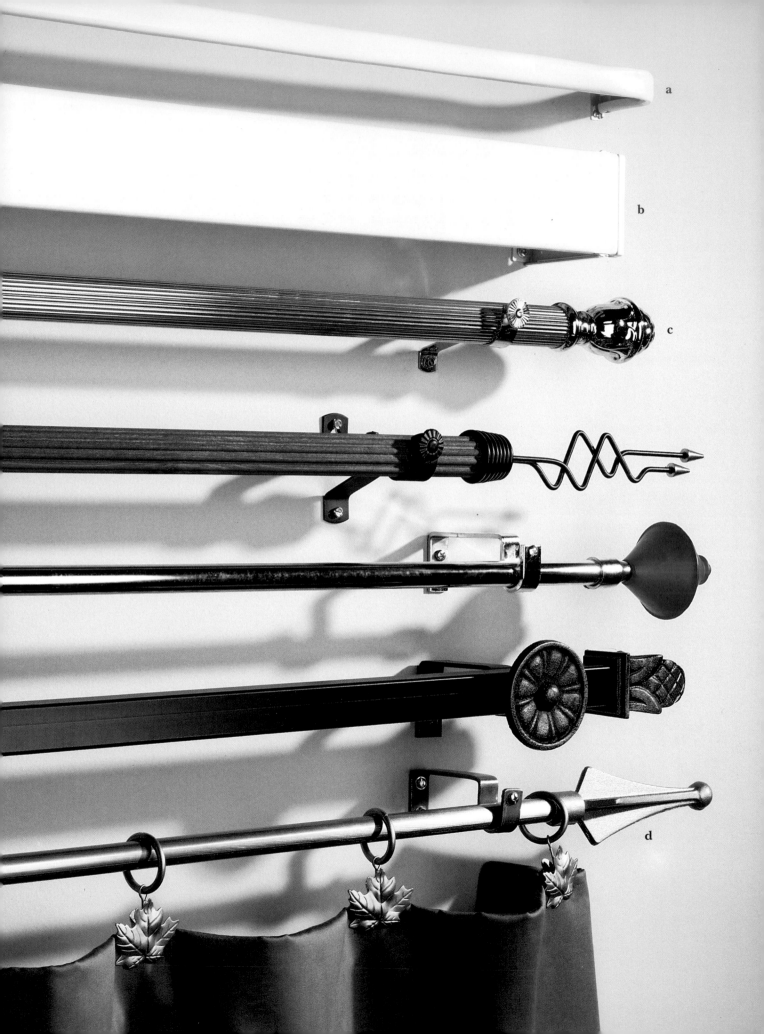

a

b

c

d

Selecting & Installing Hardware

Window treatment hardware is available in a wide range of styles to suit any decorating plan. Consider both decorative and functional needs when selecting hardware. Some curtain rods are designed to be covered completely by the fabric, while others may have decorative finishes and ornate finials that enhance the treatment. Select and install the hardware before measuring for the window treatment, because the cut length of the fabric will vary depending on the hardware placement.

Window treatment hardware is packaged complete with mounting brackets, screws or nails, and installation instructions. Use screws alone if installing through drywall or plaster directly into wall studs. When brackets are positioned between wall studs, support the screws for lightweight treatments with plastic anchors in the correct size for the screws. If the brackets must support a heavy window treatment, use plastic toggle anchors in the correct size for the wallboard depth, or use molly bolts. If nails are supplied with the hardware, use them only for lightweight treatments installed directly to the window frame. Otherwise, substitute screws or molly bolts that fit through the holes in the brackets.

Conventional and decorative drapery rods (opposite) are available in many styles. Window treatments that have a rod pocket (page 11) may be mounted on narrow curtain rods **(a)** or wide curtain rods **(b),** which are available in either 2½" (6.5 cm) or 4½" (11.5 cm) widths. Decorative metal rods and wood poles with ornate finials **(c)** are suitable for treatment styles that reveal all or part of the rod, such as tab curtains. They may be used with decorative rings **(d),** which are sewn or clipped to the top of a curtain panel. Decorative tieback holders and holdbacks (above) are stylish accessories for holding curtains back from the window.

How to Install Brackets Using Plastic Anchors

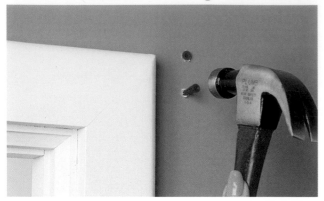

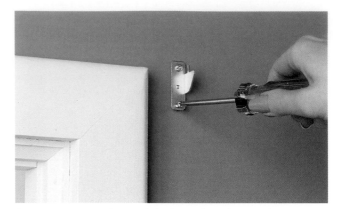

1) Mark screw locations on wall. Drill holes for plastic anchors, using drill bit slightly smaller than diameter of plastic anchor. Tap anchors into drilled holes, using hammer.

2) Insert screw through hole in bracket and into installed plastic anchor. Tighten screw securely; anchor expands in drywall, preventing it from pulling out of wall.

How to Install Brackets Using Plastic Toggle Anchors

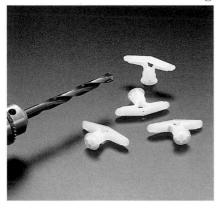

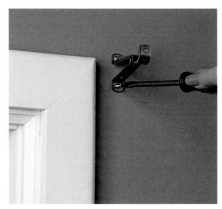

1) Mark screw locations on wall. Drill holes for plastic toggle anchors, using drill bit slightly smaller than diameter of toggle anchor shank.

2) Squeeze wings of toggle anchor flat, and push toggle anchor into hole; tap in with hammer until it is flush with wall.

3) Insert screw through hole in bracket and into installed anchor; tighten screw. Wings spread out and flatten against the back side of drywall.

How to Install Brackets Using Molly Bolts

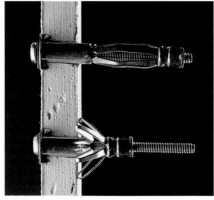

1) Mark screw locations on wall. Drill holes for molly bolts, using drill bit slightly smaller than the diameter of molly bolt.

2) Tap molly bolt into drilled hole, using hammer; tighten screw. Molly bolt expands and flattens against back side of drywall.

3) Remove screw from molly bolt; insert the screw through hole in bracket and into installed molly bolt. Screw the bracket securely in place.

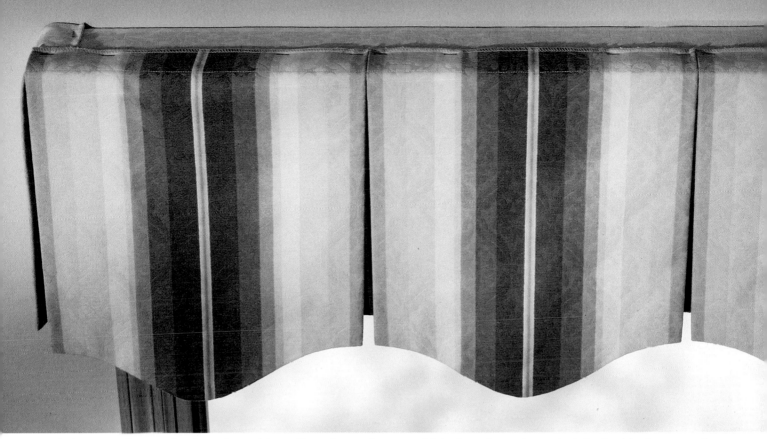

Fabric-covered mounting board provides a firm, flat surface, to which the valance is stapled. It also blocks upward light and prevents dust from falling on any existing undertreatment.

Covering & Installing Mounting Boards

Many window treatments, including Roman shades and a variety of valance styles, are mounted on boards, rather than on drapery hardware. The mounting board is covered with fabric to match the window treatment or with drapery lining, and the window treatment is then stapled to the board. The treatment may be installed as an outside mount, securing it to the window frame or to the wall above the window frame. For an inside mount, the treatment is installed inside the upper window frame, flush with the front of the frame.

The size of the mounting board varies, depending on whether the board-mounted window treatment is an inside or outside mount and whether it is being used alone or with an undertreatment. When using stock, or nominal, lumber, keep in mind that the actual measurement differs from the nominal measurement. A 1 × 2 board measures ¾" × 1½" (2 × 3.8 cm), a 1 × 4 measures ¾" × 3½" (2 × 9 cm), a 1 × 6 measures ¾" × 5½" (2 × 14 cm), and a 1 × 8 measures ¾" × 7¼" (2 × 18.7 cm).

For an inside-mounted window treatment, the depth of the window frame must be at least 1½" (3.8 cm), to accommodate a 1 × 2 mounting board. Cut the mounting board ½" (1.3 cm) shorter than the inside measurement across the window frame, to ensure that the board will fit inside the frame after it is covered with fabric.

The projection (page 11) necessary for an outside-mounted top treatment depends on the projection of any existing undertreatment. If the undertreatment is stationary, allow at least 2" (5 cm) of clearance between it and the top treatment; if the undertreatment traverses, allow at least 3" (7.5 cm) of clearance. If there is no undertreatment or if the undertreatment is mounted inside the window frame, use a 1 × 4 board for the top treatment. Cut the mounting board at least 2" (5 cm) wider than the outside width of the window frame. Install the board using angle irons that measure more than one-half the projection of the board.

For an outside-mounted Roman shade, use a 1 × 2 board, cut 2" (5 cm) longer than the outside width of the window frame. Attach the board flat to the wall for a ¾" (2 cm) projection. This allows the shade to rest close to the window frame for optimum light control and privacy.

✂ Cutting Directions

Cut the fabric to cover the mounting board, with the width of the fabric equal to the distance around the board plus 1" (2.5 cm) and the length of the fabric equal to the length of the board plus 3" (7.5 cm).

How to Cover the Mounting Board with Fabric

1) Center board on wrong side of fabric. Staple one long edge of fabric to board, placing staples about 8" (20.5 cm) apart; do not staple within 6" (15 cm) of ends. Wrap fabric around board. Fold under ⅜" (1 cm) on long edge; staple to board, placing staples about 6" (15 cm) apart.

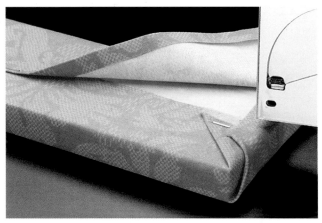

2) Miter fabric at corners on side of the board with unfolded fabric edge; finger-press. Staple miters in place near raw edge.

3) Miter fabric at corners on side of the board with folded fabric edge; finger-press. Fold under excess fabric at ends; staple near fold.

How to Install an Inside-mounted Board

1) Cover mounting board (above). Attach window treatment to mounting board. Hold board in place against upper window frame, with wide side of board up; align front edge to frame.

2) Predrill screw holes through the board and up into window frame, using ⅛" drill bit; drill holes within 1" (2.5 cm) of each end of board and in center for wide window treatments. Adjust the placement of holes to avoid screw eyes, if any. Secure board, using 8 × 1½" (3.8 cm) round-head screws.

How to Install an Outside-mounted Board

1) Cover mounting board (opposite). Attach window treatment to board. Mark screw holes for angle irons on bottom of board, positioning angle irons within 1" (2.5 cm) of each end of board and at 45" (115 cm) intervals or less.

2) Predrill screw holes into the board; size of drill bit depends on screw size required for angle iron. Screw angle irons to board.

3) Hold board at desired placement, making sure it is level; mark screw holes on wall or window frame. Remove angle irons from board.

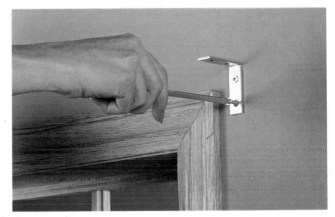

4) Secure angle irons to the wall, using 1½" (3.8 cm) flat-head screws, into wall studs; if angle irons are not positioned at wall studs, use molly bolts or toggle anchors instead of flat-head screws.

5) Reposition window treatment on angle irons, aligning screw holes; fasten screws.

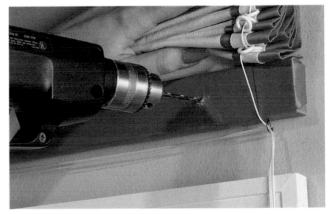

Roman shade mounted with ¾" (2 cm) projection. Install board flat to wall at desired location above window, predrilling holes through board into wall. Secure with 8 × 2½" (6.5 cm) flat-head screws into wall studs, if possible; or use molly bolts or toggle anchors if not screwing into wall studs.

Roman Shades

Banded Roman Shades

These flat Roman shades have a sleek appearance that can blend well in many decorating plans. For an eye-catching accent, bands of contrasting or coordinating fabric are sewn around the outer edges. A band width of 3" to 4" (7.5 to 10 cm) works well in proportion to the folds of the shade. The shades may be lined for added body and light control.

A flat metal weight bar, sold in hardware stores, is inserted between the band and the shade fabric at the lower edge, for stability and ease of operation. The shade may be mounted inside or outside the window frame as desired.

Flat bias edging (page 114) accents the inner edge of the banding in a contemporary Roman shade while repeating the color of the awning valance (page 66).

✂ Cutting Directions

Determine the desired finished length and width of the shade. Cut the fabric to the finished length of the shade plus the projection of the mounting board plus 1/2" (1.3 cm) for the lower seam allowance. The cut width of the shade is equal to the finished width plus 1" (2.5 cm) for side seam allowances. If more than one width of fabric is required for the shade, use one complete width for the center panel and seam equal partial widths to each side of the center panel. If lining is desired, cut the lining fabric to the same length and width as the outer fabric. Cut a strip of fabric to cover the mounting board (page 19).

Cut fabric strips for the banded edges, with the cut width of the strips 1" (2.5 cm) wider than the desired finished width of the band. For the side bands, the cut length of the fabric strips is equal to the cut length of the shade. For the lower band, the cut length of the fabric strip is equal to the cut width of the shade.

YOU WILL NEED

Decorator fabric.

Contrasting fabric, for banding and optional bias edging.

Lining fabric, optional.

1/2" (1.3 cm) plastic rings, number as determined in diagram on page 26.

Staple gun and staples.

Screw eyes, one for each vertical row of rings.

Shade cord; fabric glue.

1/2" (1.3 cm) flat metal weight bar, cut 1/2" (1.3 cm) shorter than finished width of shade.

1 × 2 mounting board, cut to desired finished width of shade.

Drill and drill bits.

#8 × 2 1/2" (6.5 cm) flat-head screws, for installing shade into wall studs; or molly bolts or toggle anchors, for installing shade into drywall or plaster.

#8 × 1 1/2" (3.8 cm) flat-head screws, for installing an inside-mounted shade.

Awning cleat; screws.

How to Make a Diagram of the Shade

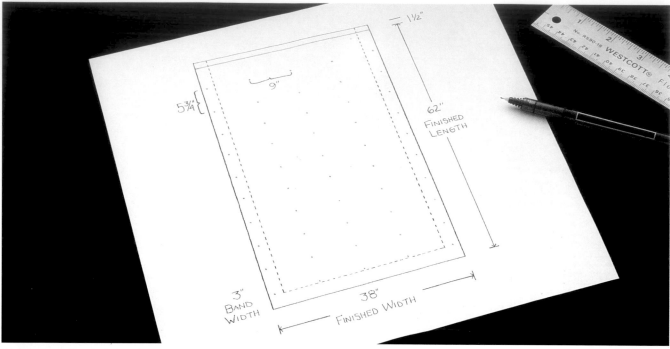

1) Diagram back side of shade, indicating finished length and width of shade and width of band. Plan locations of rings in vertical rows spaced 8" to 12" (20.5 to 30.5 cm) apart, with outer rows of rings 1" (2.5 cm) from outer edges of shade. Arrange rings in evenly spaced horizontal rows, 5" to 8" (12.5 to 20.5 cm) apart, with bottom row at top stitching line of band, and top row a distance from the top of the shade equal to the distance between rings.

How to Sew a Banded Roman Shade

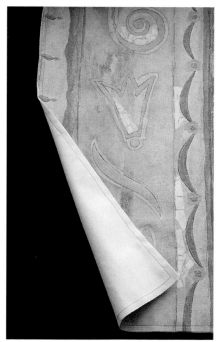

1) Seam the fabric widths together, if necessary. For a lined shade, pin the lining to the outer fabric, wrong sides together, matching the raw edges; machine baste ⅜" (1 cm) from raw edges.

2) Plain banding. Press under ½" (1.3 cm) on one long edge of each banding strip.

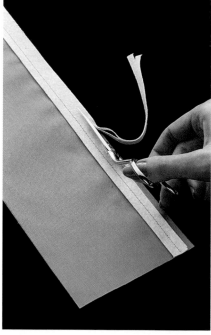

2) Banding with flat bias edging. Prepare edging as on page 114, steps 1 and 2. Sew edging to one long side of each banding strip, as on page 115, steps 3 and 4. Press seam allowances toward banding.

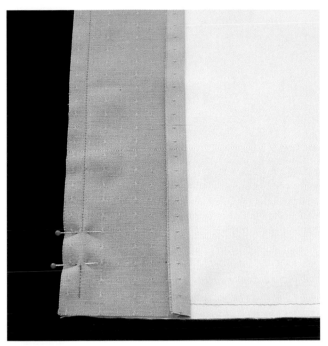

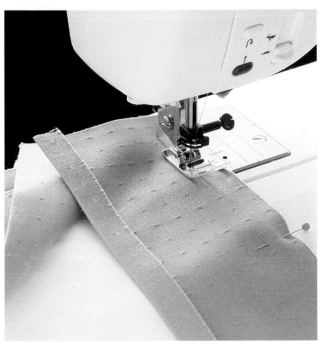

3) Pin one side band to shade panel, with right side of band to wrong side of panel, aligning raw edges. Stitch ½" (1.3 cm) seam, starting and stopping ½" (1.3 cm) from side edges. Repeat for opposite side, leaving 1" (2.5 cm) opening 1" (2.5 cm) above end of stitching line.

4) Pin lower band to lower edge of shade; stitch ½" (1.3 cm) seam, starting and stopping ½" (1.3 cm) from side edges.

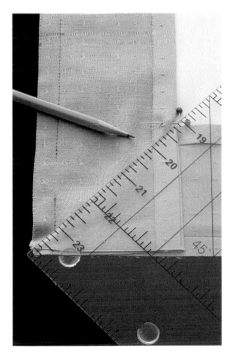

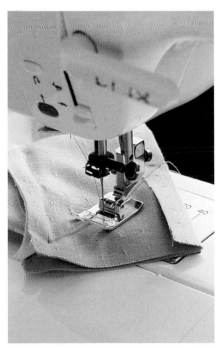

5) Mark band for mitering, placing pins at the inner corner as shown. Draw lines from inner corners of the banding to stitched corners, at 45° angle.

6) Stitch miter on marked line from inner corner to end of stitching at outer corner; take care not to catch shade panel in stitching.

7) Trim the mitered seams to ½" (1.3 cm), and press open. Trim the corners diagonally. Press the seam allowance of band toward band, using tip of iron.

(Continued on next page)

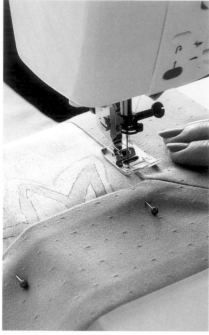

8) Plain banding. Turn band to the right side of shade; press the band, with seamline on outer edge of the shade. Pin band in place. Topstitch around band, close to inner edge.

8) Banding with flat bias edging. Turn band to right side of shade; press band, with seamline on outer edge of the shade. Pin the band in place. Stitch in the ditch of the seam between banding and edging.

9) Finish upper edge of shade, using zigzag or overlock stitch. Place shade facedown on flat surface. Mark a line a distance from finished edge equal to the projection of the mounting board, indicating top of shade.

10) Mark locations for rings as determined in diagram. If shade is lined, pin through both layers of fabric at center of ring markings, with pins parallel to bottom of shade. Fold shade in accordion pleats at marks, to position shade for attaching rings.

11) Attach rings by machine or by hand, as in step 7 on page 33 or 34. Cover mounting board (page 20). Align upper edge of shade to back of top edge of mounting board; staple shade to mounting board.

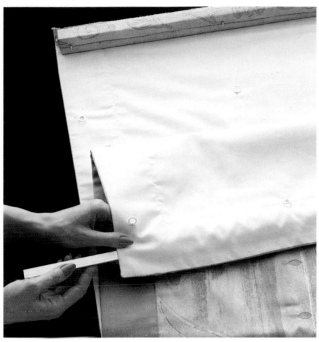

12) **Install** screw eyes on narrow underside of mounting board, aligning them to rows of rings. Insert flat weight bar into opening near lower corner; stitch opening closed.

13) **Place** the shade facedown on flat surface. Decide whether the draw cord will hang on left or right side of shade. String first row of rings opposite the draw side. Run cord through rings from bottom to top and across shade through screw eyes; extend cord desired distance down draw side of shade.

14) **Cut** and tie cord for first row securely at bottom ring. String remaining rows, running cord through each succeeding row of rings and through screw eyes; cut and tie each cord at bottom ring. Apply fabric glue to knots, to prevent them from fraying or becoming untied.

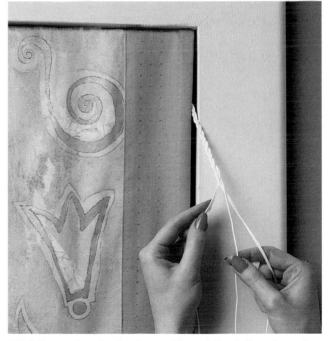

15) **Mount** the shade (page 20 or 21). Adjust length of cords, with shade lowered so the tension on all cords is equal. Tie cords together just below screw eye. Braid cords to desired length; knot. Complete shade, following step 14 on page 35.

Butterfly Roman Shades

This simple, yet stylish, window treatment has the sleek smoothness of a flat Roman shade, with draped softness at the lower edge. Excess length is folded up and secured, forming a swag at the lower hem when the shade is down. As the shade is drawn up, the folds stack in the center and flare at the sides, creating a butterfly effect. The shade is lined to give it extra body and protect the fabric from sunlight. A dowel, inserted into a pocket in the lining, adds stability to the shade.

This Roman shade style works best if the finished width does not exceed 49½" (126.3 cm). A shade of this width can be made from 54" (137 cm) fabric, with no seaming necessary. Plan to mount the shade above the window frame, so that the finished length from the top of the mounting board to the highest point of the hem is evenly divisible by six.

✂ Cutting Directions

Cut the decorator fabric with the length equal to the desired finished length of the shade plus 26¾" (68 cm); this allows for the bottom swag, hem allowance, and mounting. The cut width of the decorator fabric is equal to the desired finished width of the shade plus 4½" (11.5 cm); this allows for double ¾" (2 cm) side hems and twice the ¾" (2 cm) projection of the mounting board. Cut a strip of decorator fabric to cover the mounting board (page 19).

Cut the lining fabric with the length equal to the cut length of the decorator fabric plus 1¼" (3.2 cm) and the width equal to the desired finished width of the shade plus 1½" (3.8 cm).

YOU WILL NEED

Decorator fabric.

Lining fabric.

⅜" (1 cm) wooden dowel, with length equal to two-thirds the finished shade width minus ½" (1.3 cm).

½" (1.3 cm) plastic rings, number as determined in diagram on page 32.

1 × 2 mounting board, cut to desired finished width of shade.

Staple gun and staples.

Three screw eyes.

Shade cord; fabric glue; drapery pull.

Drill and drill bits.

8 × 2½" (6.5 cm) flat-head screws, for installing shade into wall studs; or molly bolts or toggle anchors, for installing shade into drywall or plaster.

Awning cleat; screws.

How to Make a Diagram of the Shade

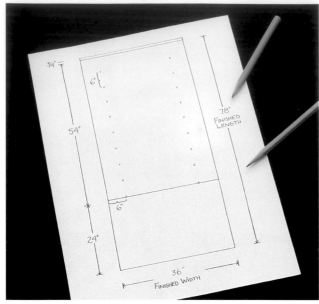 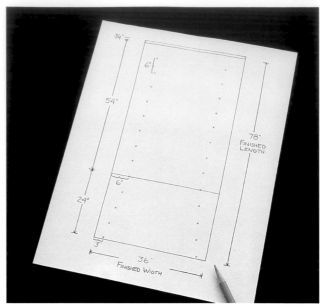

1) Diagram back side of the shade, indicating ring placement marks. Draw a line 24" (61 cm) from the bottom of the shade, indicating the dowel pocket. Plan two vertical rows of rings from the dowel pocket to 6¾" (17 cm) from top of shade, each positioned one-sixth of the shade width from the hemmed sides; space rings 6" (15 cm) apart vertically.

2) Mark positions for two rings in center of the lower hem, each a distance from outer edge equal to one-sixth of the shade width minus 3" (7.5 cm). Remaining three rings in each row are spaced evenly along a line between dowel pocket ring and lower ring.

How to Sew a Butterfly Roman Shade

1) Mark line across lining 26⅝" (67.5 cm) from the lower cut edge. Fold the lining, right sides together, along the marked line; pin. Stitch ⅝" (1.5 cm) from the fold, forming dowel pocket. Press pocket toward lower edge.

2) Insert dowel into dowel pocket and slide it to center of lining; tack through dowel pocket to hold the dowel in place.

3) Press under ¾" (2 cm) twice on sides of shade fabric. Place lining over shade fabric, wrong sides together, matching upper and lower edges; at sides, place lining under hems, up to second foldline.

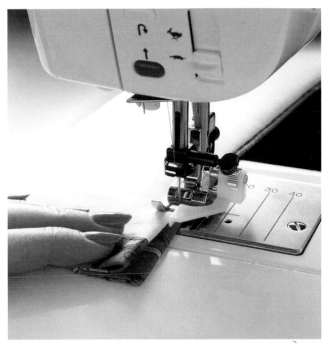

4) Pin side hems to lining; blindstitch in place. Press under 1" (2.5 cm) of lining and shade fabric twice at lower edge; pin. Blindstitch in place.

5) Finish upper edge of shade and lining together, using overlock or zigzag stitch. Place shade facedown on flat surface. Mark a line ¾" (2 cm) from finished upper edge, indicating top of shade. Mark locations for rings, as determined in diagram; place marks for rings at ends of dowel, on dowel pocket stitching line.

6) Pin through both layers of fabric at center of ring markings, with pins parallel to bottom of shade. Fold shade in accordion pleats at pins, to position shade for attaching rings.

7) Attaching rings by machine. Attach rings by placing fold under the presser foot with ring next to fold at mark. Set zigzag stitch at widest setting; set stitch length at 0. Stitch over ring, securing it with about eight stitches. Secure the stitches by stitching in place for two or three stitches, with stitch width and length set at 0.

(Continued on next page)

7) Attaching rings by hand. Tack rings by hand, using double strand of thread, stitching in place through both fabric layers for four or five stitches.

8) Cover mounting board (page 20). Align upper edge of shade to the back of narrow top edge of mounting board, centering shade on board so hemmed sides extend beyond board. Staple shade to the mounting board; wrap sides over ends of board, and staple in place on top of board, forming squared corners.

9) Decide whether draw cord will hang on left or right side of shade. Install screw eyes on the narrow underside of mounting board, aligning two of them to rows of rings; install third screw eye 1" (2.5 cm) from end of board on draw side.

10) Place shade facedown on flat surface. String first row of rings, opposite the draw side. Run the cord through rings from bottom to top and across the shade through three screw eyes; extend cord about halfway down draw side of shade.

11) String remaining row of rings, running the cord through two screw eyes and extending cord about halfway down draw side. Tie lower five rings of each row together securely. Apply fabric glue to knot and end of cord to prevent knot from slipping.

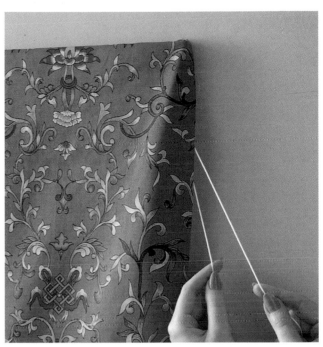

12) Mount the shade above the window, following instructions for the Roman shade with ¾" (2 cm) projection on page 21. Adjust length of cords, with shade lowered, so the tension on both cords is equal. Tie cords together just below screw eye.

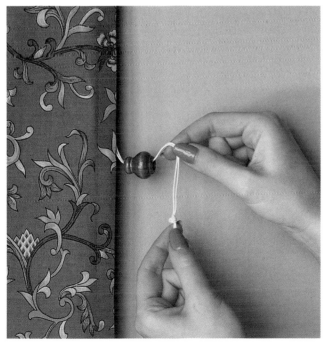

13) Insert ends of the cord into top of the drapery pull; knot ends.

14) Screw awning cleat into window frame or wall. When shade is raised, wrap cord around the awning cleat to hold at desired height.

Mock Rod-mounted Roman Shades

This version of a flat Roman shade appears to be suspended from a decorative rod mounted over the window. In reality, the shade is attached by hook and loop tape to a mounting board that also carries the screw eyes for raising and lowering the shade.

Decorative cording is laced from the rod through grommets at the top of the shade, giving it a nautical look. For added embellishment, flat braid or trim can be sewn onto the surface of the shade before the rings are attached.

Select a rod that has a minimal projection so that the shade can rest as close as possible to the window. Select a mounting board of stock lumber in a width to match the projection of the rod, or cut one to size.

✂ Cutting Directions

Determine the desired length and width of the shade with the upper edge 3" (7.5 cm) above the window frame. Outer edges should extend at least 1" (2.5 cm) beyond the sides of the window frame. Cut the fabric to the finished length of the shade plus 7" (18 cm). The cut width of the fabric is equal to the finished width of the shade plus 4" (10 cm).

Cut the lining fabric with the length and width equal to the finished length and width of the shade.

Cut a strip of fabric to cover the mounting board (page 19).

YOU WILL NEED

Decorator fabric.

Lining fabric.

Hook and loop tape, ¾" (2 cm) wide, with length equal to finished width of shade.

Flat braid or other decorative trim, optional.

½" (1.3 cm) plastic rings, number as determined in diagram on page 38.

Grommets and attaching tool in size suitable for cording.

Staple gun and staples.

Screw eyes, one for each vertical row of rings.

Shade cord; fabric glue.

½" (1.3 cm) flat metal weight bar, cut ½" (1.3 cm) shorter than finished width of shade.

Mounting board with projection to match decorative rod, cut to desired finished width of shade.

Drill and drill bits.

Two angle irons that measure more than one-half the projection of the mounting board, 1½" (3.8 cm) flat-head screws for installing angle irons into wall studs; or molly bolts or toggle anchors, for installing angle irons into drywall or plaster.

Decorative rod with shallow projection.

Decorative cording; metal endcaps, optional.

Awning cleat; screws.

How to Make a Diagram of the Shade

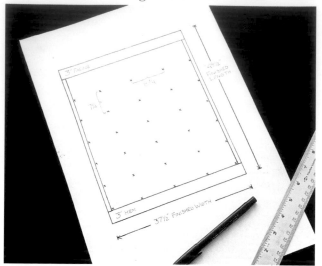

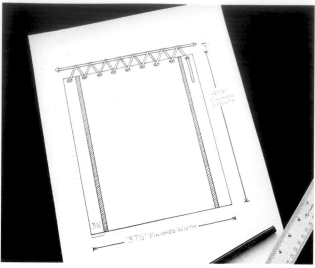

1) Diagram back side of shade, indicating finished length and width. Plan locations of rings in vertical rows spaced 8" to 12" (20.5 to 30.5 cm) apart, with outer rows of rings 1" (2.5 cm) from outer edges of shade. Arrange rings in evenly spaced horizontal rows, 5" to 8" (12.5 to 20.5 cm) apart, with bottom row at stitching line of hem pocket, and top row a distance from the facing stitching line equal to the distance between rings.

2) Diagram front side of shade, planning placement of any flat braids or trims. Plan placement of the rod, number and spacing of grommets in the upper faced edge, and manner in which the cord will be laced.

How to Sew a Mock Rod-mounted Roman Shade

1) Embellish right side of shade fabric with flat braid or other decorative trim, as determined in diagram; allow 2" (5 cm) for side hems and 3½" (9 cm) at upper and lower edges for facing and hem pocket.

2) Press under 1" (2.5 cm) twice on sides of shade fabric. Place the lining over shade fabric, wrong sides together, with lower edge of lining 3½" (9 cm) above lower edge of shade fabric; at sides, place the lining under hems, up to second foldline.

3) Pin side hems; blindstitch in place. Press under ½" (1.3 cm) at lower edge; then press under 3" (7.5 cm), to make hem pocket. Stitch close to first fold.

4) Press under ½" (1.3 cm) at upper edge; then press under 3" (7.5 cm), to form facing. Align edge of loop tape to lower foldline; glue-baste tape in place.

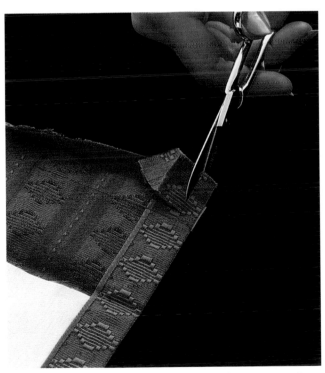

5) Unfold facing. Stitch along edge of tape opposite foldline. Trim out excess layers of fabric at corners.

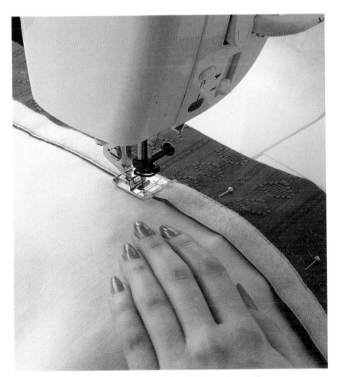

6) Refold facing; pin. Stitch facing along lower foldline, stitching through edge of loop tape.

(Continued on next page)

7) Mark locations for rings, as determined in the diagram (page 38). Follow steps 6 and 7 on pages 33 and 34 for attaching rings.

8) Fasten grommets, using attaching tool; position grommets as determined in diagram on page 38, with upper edge of grommets at least ½" (1.3 cm) below upper edge of panel.

9) Cover mounting board (page 20). Staple hook tape to narrow front edge of board. Install angle iron within 1" (2.5 cm) of each end (page 21). Hold the board, wide side up, just above window; mark line on underside of board even with front edge of window frame. Mark screw holes on wall.

10) Remove angle irons from board; install on wall. Install screw eyes on the wide underside of mounting board, between front edge of board and marked line, aligning them to rows of rings.

11) Insert flat weight bar into hem pocket; stitch openings closed. Affix mounting board to shade along hook and loop tape.

12) Follow steps 13 and 14 on page 29. Reposition the shade on angle irons, aligning the screw holes; fasten screws.

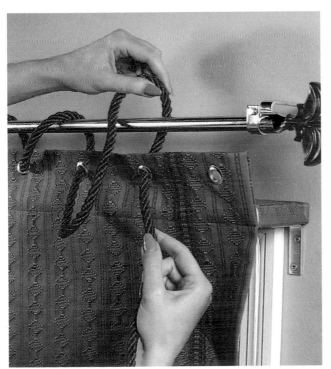

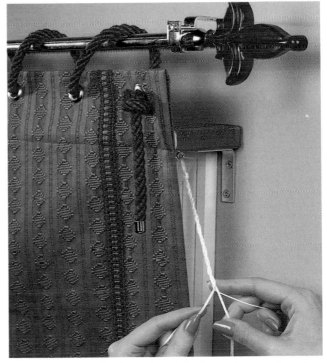

13) Install decorative rod the desired distance above top of shade. Lace the cording over rod and through grommets as desired; knot ends. Secure metal end caps to cord ends, or make self tassels (page 124).

14) Adjust length of cords, with shade lowered so the tension on all cords is equal. Tie cords together just below screw eye. Braid cords to desired length; knot. Follow step 14 on page 35.

Layered Valances

A basic rod-pocket valance can have a more decorative, custom look, simply by adding a petticoat. The petticoat, or underlayer, is made of a contrasting or coordinating fabric that peeks out 1½" to 2" (3.8 to 5 cm) below the hem of the top layer. Both layers are sewn together into one rod pocket and heading and gathered onto a curtain rod.

Either or both layers may be lined, depending on the type of fabric used and the degree to which light shines through them. Layer the fabrics right sides up, and hold them in front of the window to decide whether lining is necessary. If the underlayer has a pattern that shows through to the top layer, it may be necessary to line the top layer. If a uniform white appearance is desired from the outside of the window, the underlayer may be lined also.

When selecting fabrics for layered valances, keep in mind that the layers tend to get quite thick at the side hems and along the rod pocket, especially if lining is required. Select lightweight fabric for one or both

layers, if possible. Lace or eyelet valance fabric with a finished lower edge may be used for the underlayer, giving the valance a feminine accent and eliminating the need for lining.

The size and style of curtain rod that is used can greatly affect the finished appearance of the valance. Wide rods that measure 2½" or 4" (6.5 or 10 cm) can be used to create a bolder look and can accommodate higher headings, if desired. Wide rods are also available in an arch shape that raises the center of the valance.

YOU WILL NEED

Decorator fabric, for upper layer.

Contrasting or coordinating decorator fabric, or lace or eyelet valance fabric, for underlayer.

Lining fabric, optional.

Curtain rod.

Lace petticoat underlayer (opposite) gives an arched layered valance a feminine accent. The striped companion fabric (above), used as the underlayer, brings out the colors of the flowered upper layer.

Cutting Directions

Determine the depths of the rod pocket and the heading (page 11). Then determine the finished width and the desired finished length of each layer from the top of the heading to the hem.

Cut fabric for the upper layer, with the cut length equal to the desired finished length plus the heading depth plus the rod-pocket depth plus ½" (1.3 cm) for turn-under at the upper edge plus 4" (10 cm) for a double 2" (5 cm) hem. Cut enough widths of fabric to equal the finished width, including the returns, multiplied by two to two-and-one-half times fullness.

Cut fabric for the underlayer, with the cut length equal to the desired finished length plus 4" (10 cm). The cut width of the underlayer is equal to the cut width of the upper layer. If only one layer is to be lined, the cut width of the lined layer is equal to the total width of the other layer after seaming and hemming plus 1" (2.5 cm).

If lining is desired, cut the lining fabric with the cut length equal to the desired finished length of the layer and the cut width equal to the cut width of the layer.

For a lace or eyelet underlayer, cut the valance fabric with the cut length equal to the desired finished length and the cut width equal to the total width of the upper layer after seaming and hemming plus 2" (5 cm).

How to Sew an Unlined Layered Valance

1) Seam fabric widths for each layer. Check to see that seamed layers are exactly the same width; cut off excess, if necessary.

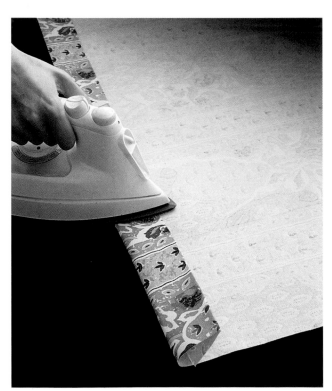

2) Press under 2" (5 cm) twice at lower edge of one layer; pin. Stitch, using straight stitch or blindstitch.

3) Press under 1" (2.5 cm) twice on sides of layer; pin. Stitch, using straight stitch or blindstitch.

4) **Repeat** steps 2 and 3 for remaining layer.

5) **Press** under ½" (1.3 cm) on upper edge of upper layer. Then press under an amount equal to rod-pocket depth plus heading depth.

6) **Place** upper layer facedown on flat surface; open out upper fold. Place underlayer facedown over upper layer, aligning upper edge of underlayer to foldline on upper layer. Refold upper edge of upper layer, encasing upper edge of underlayer; pin.

7) **Stitch** close to first fold; stitch again at depth of heading, using tape on bed of sewing machine as stitching guide. Insert the rod through rod pocket, distributing fullness evenly; mount rod on brackets.

How to Sew a Lined Layered Valance

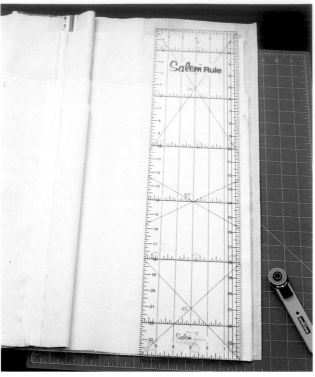

1) Seam the fabric and lining widths for each layer. Check to see that all seamed layers are exactly the same width; cut off excess, if necessary.

2) Pin one layer and its lining, right sides together, along lower edge. Stitch 2" (5 cm) from raw edges.

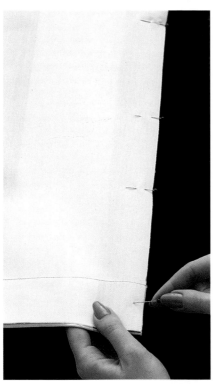

3) Press 2" (5 cm) hem allowance away from lining. Pin layer to lining along sides, aligning upper edges; layer will form fold even with lower edge of hem allowance.

4) Stitch ½" (1.3 cm) side seams. Clip the lower corners diagonally. Press lining seam allowances toward the lining. Turn the layer right side out; press.

5) Repeat steps 2 to 4 for remaining layer. Complete valance as on page 47, steps 5 to 7.

How to Sew a Layered Valance with One Lined Layer

1) Seam the fabric widths and lining widths for both layers. Hem lower edge and sides of unlined layer as on page 46, steps 2 and 3. Trim the seamed widths of decorator fabric and lining for lined layer, with width equal to the hemmed width of the unlined layer plus 1" (2.5 cm).

2) Follow steps 2 to 4, opposite, for lined layer. Complete valance as on page 47, steps 5 to 7.

How to Sew a Layered Valance with a Lace or Eyelet Underlayer

1) Seam fabric and lining, if any, for the upper layer; trim to the exact same width. Prepare upper layer, following steps 2 and 3 for unlined valance or steps 2 to 4 for lined valance. Cut lace or eyelet valance fabric 2" (5 cm) wider than prepared upper layer.

2) Press under ½" (1.3 cm) twice on the sides of the underlayer; pin. Stitch, using straight stitch. Complete valance as on page 47, steps 5 to 7.

Gathered Pickup Valances

A gathered pickup valance looks quite complicated, but is actually fairly easy to sew. The valance is basically a flat, lined rectangle with a rod pocket and heading, gathered onto a rod. At evenly spaced intervals, vertical rows of tucks are sewn into the valance, drawing the lower section of the valance up into graceful bells. The fabric between the bells falls into gentle swags. Welting at the lower edge accents and supports the curves of the bells and swags. A contrasting fabric, used to line the valance, peeks out from the inside of each bell. If desired, the valance may be interlined with flannel for added body and a slightly padded appearance.

When planning the layout of the valance, work with enough full or half widths of fabric to equal about

two-and-one-half times fullness. Bells are positioned at each seam and at each midpoint between seams. Though it is generally not desirable to position prominent details of a window treatment at the seam, this pattern of placement coincides with the placement pattern of large motifs in most decorator fabrics, allowing primary motifs to fall in the center of each swag.

The valance hangs straight down at the returns, to a length that is about 6" (15 cm) longer than the length at the center of each swag. The shortest point

at the back of each bell is about 2" (5 cm) shorter than the swags.

YOU WILL NEED

Decorator fabric, for valance.

Decorator fabric, for contrast lining.

Fabric-covered welting, twisted welting, or ½" (1.3 cm) cord and fabric, for making fabric-covered welting.

Flannel interlining, optional.

Curtain rod in desired size.

✂ Cutting Directions

Determine the desired finished length at the side of the valance from the top of the heading to the welting. The cut length of the valance fabric is equal to the desired finished length plus the depth of the heading plus the depth of the rod pocket, plus 1" (2.5 cm) for turn-under at the lower edge of the rod pocket and the lower seam allowance.

Determine the desired finished width of the valance plus two returns. Multiply this amount by two-and-one-half times fullness. Divide this amount by the fabric width and round up or down to the nearest whole or half width, to determine the number of fabric widths needed.

Cut the fabric for the contrast lining to the same length and width as the valance fabric.

If interlining is desired, the cut width of the interlining fabric is equal to the total width of the valance fabric after seaming. The cut length of the interlining fabric is equal to the finished length of the valance. If possible, railroad (page 12) the interlining to avoid seams.

Cut bias fabric strips if making fabric-covered welting, following step 1 on page 111.

Fabric with Large Motifs. Before cutting the fabric, consider the position of the primary motifs in the fabric and where they will fall in the finished valance. Avoid positioning them toward the top of the valance where they will be obscured by the gathers of the rod pocket or the tucks above the bell. Rather, make the cuts with the primary motifs centered vertically in the lower 12" to 15" (30.5 to 38 cm), so they will be more visible in the finished valance.

In fabrics with large motifs (below), one complete vertical repeat will have two rows of motifs with staggered placement. One row will have two full motifs, while the second row will have one full motif in the center and two halves of another motif matching at the selvages. The large motifs may be separated by open space or secondary motifs. Plan the cutting line for the lower edge of the valance under the row with two full motifs, so that the motifs will fall in the swags of the valance.

One vertical repeat

Cutting line for lower edge

How to Sew a Gathered Pickup Valance

1) Seam valance fabric widths. Repeat for contrast lining. Check to see that valance and lining are exactly the same width and length.

2) Make fabric-covered welting (page 111) and attach it to lower edge of valance, if desired; begin and end welting ½" (1.3 cm) from the side edges. Or, attach purchased welting (page 113). For valance without interlining, omit step 3.

3) Seam interlining, if necessary. Pin interlining to wrong side of lining along sides, with lower edge of interlining ½" (1.3 cm) above lower edge of lining. Baste within ½" (1.3 cm) seam allowances on sides.

4) Place the valance and lining right sides together, matching raw edges; pin along sides and lower edge. Stitch ½" (1.3 cm) seams on sides and lower edge, using zipper foot and stitching with valance fabric on top. Along lower edge, stitch inside the previous stitching line, crowding stitches against welting.

(Continued on next page)

5) Clip lower corners diagonally. Turn valance right side out. Press sides and lower edges. If valance is interlined, smooth interlining in place, checking to see that upper edge of interlining stops a distance from upper edge of valance equal to heading depth plus rod pocket depth plus ½" (1.3 cm).

6) Press under ½" (1.3 cm) on upper edge, turning under valance and lining together. Then press under an amount equal to heading depth plus rod-pocket depth; pin.

7) Stitch close to first fold; stitch again at depth of heading, using tape on bed of sewing machine as stitching guide.

8) Lay valance facedown on flat surface. Mark vertical rows of tucks at each seam and at each halfway point between seams. Distance from outer row of marks to side edge equals distance between rows. Measure up 10" (25.5 cm) from lower edge for placement of first mark in each row. Place remaining marks evenly spaced between lower mark and lower stitching line of rod pocket, dividing distance into three equal parts.

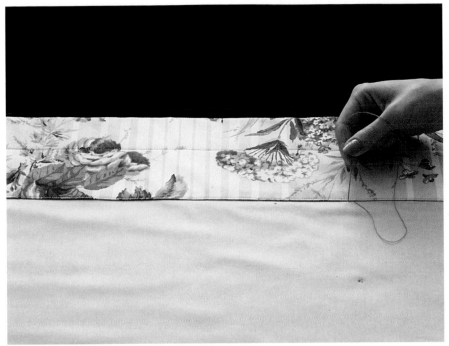

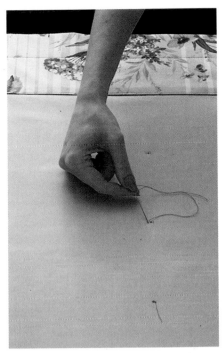

9) Thread large-eyed needle with heavy thread. Insert needle into valance at lowest mark in row. Bring needle back through to lining side of valance at next mark. Repeat, taking small stitch at each mark and running thread on right side of valance to lower stitching line of rod pocket. Insert needle ¼" (6 mm) to side of top stitch.

10) Make a second row of stitches alongside first row back to lowest mark. Cut thread, leaving tails.

11) Repeat steps 9 and 10 for each marked row. Pull up stitches to make three tucks in each row. Knot thread securely.

12) Insert rod into rod pocket. Mount rod; distribute gathers evenly. Shape bells and swags as desired.

Pleated Valances

Pleated valances offer a wide range of design possibilities, from crisply pressed tailoring to softly folded elegance. Knife pleats and box pleats are the two basic styles, with inverted box pleats offering a third alternative. Unlimited variations in pleat sizes and arrangements make it possible to design unique valances to suit any decorating scheme.

Knife pleats are commonly arranged as a series of sharp pleats of equal size and spacing, usually 1" to 2" (2.5 to 5 cm), and all turned in the same direction. For symmetry, knife-pleated valances are usually divided visually in the center, with pleats turned toward the outer edges. Pleats may be arranged continuously from the center outward, or in clusters of three or more pleats separated by spaces.

A box pleat has the appearance of two abutting knife pleats turned toward each other. Box pleats are generally deeper than knife pleats and are separated by wider spaces. A valance, such as the one on page 114, may be designed with continuous box pleats of equal size and spacing, with a pleat centered at each front corner. To vary the look, fewer box pleats may be placed farther apart, perhaps accenting existing structural divisions of the window.

For inverted box pleats, the excess fabric of the pleat is folded to the outside. This style is especially appealing when the folds are left unpressed for a softer look. If desired, a decorative trim may be applied to the lower edge of a valance with unpressed pleats.

Careful consideration must be given to the fabric for pleated valances. Pleating will obviously distort the pattern of the fabric, so smaller, all-over prints are more desirable than large prints. Striped and plaid fabrics can work very well for pleated valances as long as the pleat sizes and arrangements are planned to coincide with the fabric pattern.

A diagram of the valance will help to determine finished width and length. It is necessary to make a paper pattern of the valance, following steps 1 to 3 on page 58. The pattern will help determine pleat size, spacing, and placement of seams, allowing for adjustments before the fabric is cut. Any seams must be hidden in the folds of the pleats. If possible, the fabric may be railroaded (page 12), eliminating the need for seams.

To prevent excess bulk at the hem, pleated valances may be self-lined or lined with a lightweight fabric in an accent color. If white or off-white lining is preferred, a flat bias edging (page 114), ½" (1.3 cm) wide, may be sewn into the lower seam, preventing the lining from peeking out at the lower edge. Self-lined valances may be interlined with lightweight drapery lining, if necessary, to prevent the pattern on the back from showing through to the front.

Knife pleats in the top valance were planned to play off the plaid pattern in the fabric. Unpressed inverted box pleats (above) are edged with a tassel fringe trim.

How to Make a Pattern for the Valance

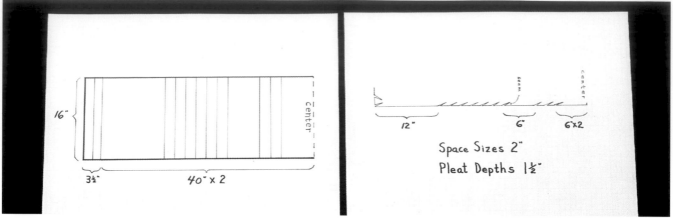

1) Diagram valance to scale on graph paper, indicating finished length, width, return depth, and desired placement of pleats. Returns of 3½" (9 cm) or more can accommodate two or more knife pleats or half of a box pleat. Avoid pleats on smaller returns. Draw an aerial view of the valance, indicating pleat depths, space sizes, and any seam placements. When planning pleat sizes and placement, avoid excess bulk of overlapping pleats. For striped or plaid valance, follow fabric pattern to determine pleat and space sizes. Check to see that space measurements add up to finished width.

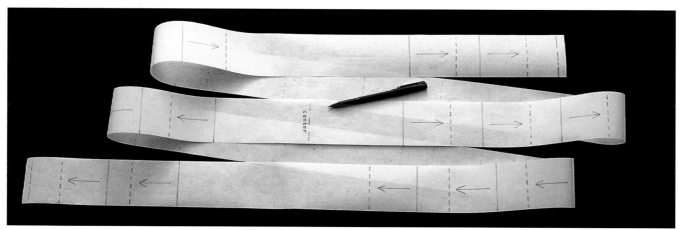

2) Unroll adding machine paper on flat surface. Mark ½" (1.3 cm) side seam allowance at end. Measure and mark all spaces and pleats as determined in step 1. Mark folds with solid lines; mark placement lines with dotted lines. Indicate direction of folds with arrows. Mark pattern for entire width of valance, ending with ½" (1.3 cm) seam allowance for opposite end; cut paper.

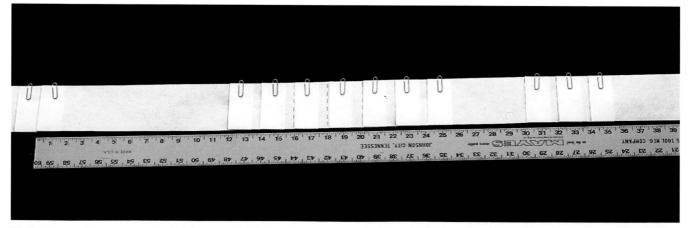

3) Fold out pleats as marked. Measure folded pattern to see that it equals desired finished width, including returns; adjust a few pleats, if necessary.

YOU WILL NEED

Graph paper.

Roll of paper, such as adding machine paper.

Decorator fabric.

Lightweight decorator fabric in accent color, for lining; or drapery lining, if valance is not self-lined.

Lightweight decorator fabric, for flat bias edging on valance lined with drapery lining.

Lightweight drapery lining, for interlining on self-lined valance, optional.

Heavy paper, for pressing pleats.

Decorative trim, for valance with unpressed pleats, optional.

Mounting board, cut to length as determined on page 19.

Angle irons with flat-head screws; length of angle iron should be more than one-half the projection of board.

8 × 2½" (6.5 cm) flat-head screws, for installing valance into wall studs; or molly bolts or toggle anchors, for installing into drywall or plaster.

Staple gun and staples.

✂ Cutting Directions

Cut the fabric for a self-lined valance with the length equal to twice the desired finished length plus 3" (7.5 cm).

Cut the fabric for a lined valance with the length equal to the desired finished length plus 2" (5 cm).

Determine the approximate cut width by measuring the total width of the pattern, opposite; allow excess width for placing seams in the folds of pleats. Cut the valance fabric to the necessary width in step 1, below.

Cut the interlining for an interlined valance with the length equal to the desired finished length of the valance plus 1½" (3.8 cm), and the width equal to the cut width of the valance fabric.

Cut the lining for a lined valance with the same length and width as the valance fabric.

Cut bias fabric strips 2" (5 cm) wide, if making a lined valance with a flat bias edging; follow step 1 on page 111.

How to Sew a Self-lined Pleated Valance

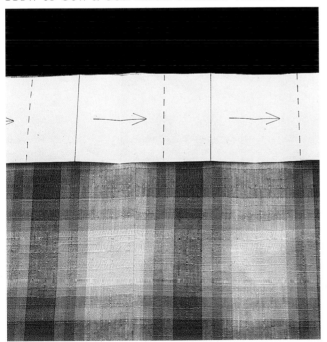

1) Seam fabric widths as necessary. Trim the seam allowances to ¼" (6 mm); press open. Lay valance pattern over seamed fabric, aligning seams to points in pattern where they will be hidden in pleats; cut fabric to width of pattern.

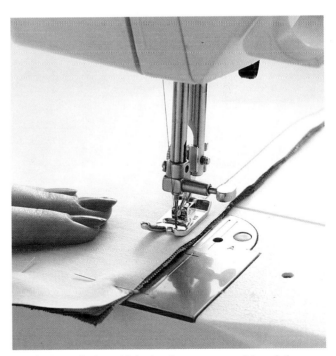

2) Pin interlining, if desired, to wrong side of the valance, matching upper edges and ends. Fold end of valance in half lengthwise, right sides together. Sew ½" (1.3 cm) seam on outer edge of the return. Repeat for opposite end of valance.

(Continued on next page)

3) Turn valance right side out; press. Match upper raw edges. The lower edge of interlining, if used, extends to lower fold of the valance. Machine-baste layers together, ½" (1.3 cm) from upper raw edges. For valance with unpressed pleats, apply trim to the lower edge (page 116), if desired.

4) Lay valance faceup on flat surface; lay pattern over upper edge of valance, aligning end seamlines to seamed outer edges. Transfer pattern markings to valance. Repeat along lower edge.

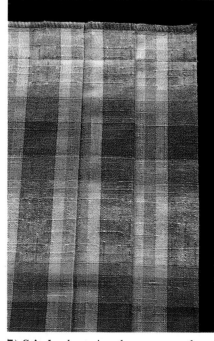

5) Pin pleats in place along upper and lower edges and center of the valance. Measure the valance width; adjust if necessary, distributing the adjustment among several pleats. If unpressed pleats are desired, omit step 6.

6) Press pleats on face of valance, removing pins from one pleat at a time; insert heavy paper under each pleat as it is pressed, to avoid imprinting. Replace pins along upper edge.

7) Stitch pleats in place across the valance, 1½" (3.8 cm) from the upper edge; remove pins. Finish the upper edge, using overlock or zigzag stitch.

8) Cover the mounting board (page 20). Position valance on mounting board, using stitching line as guide to extend upper edge 1½" (3.8 cm) onto top of board; position end pleats at front corners of the board. Staple valance in place at returns. Clip fabric at corner pleats close to stitching line to control the excess bulk. Staple valance in place; ease or stretch valance slightly to fit board, if necessary. Mount the valance (page 21).

How to Sew a Lined Pleated Valance

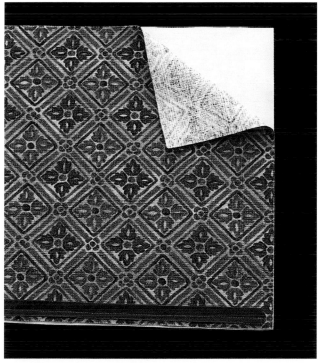

1) Follow step 1 on page 59. Cut lining to same width as valance fabric. Make flat bias edging (page 114) and attach it to lower edge of the valance, if desired; begin and end edging ½" (1.3 cm) from side edges.

2) Place valance and lining right sides together, matching raw edges; pin along sides and lower edge. Stitch ½" (1.3 cm) seams on sides and lower edge. Complete valance as in steps 3 to 8, opposite and above.

Pleated Valances with Shaped Lower Edges

For a stylish variation of the pleated valance, the lower edge can be shaped into gentle curves or angles. Valance and lining pieces are cut using a full-size pattern. The valance is then constructed following the instructions for a lined pleated valance on page 61, without the flat bias edging. Because the lining may be visible along the lower edge in some areas, it is recommended that the valance be lined in a coordinating or contrasting fabric.

The design options for the lower edge are limitless. You may copy the ideas on these pages or create others. Begin by sketching the window treatment to scale on graph paper. Perhaps shape the lower edge of the valance to accent structural details of the window itself, or repeat design lines used elsewhere in the room.

YOU WILL NEED

Graph paper.

Roll of wide paper, such as inexpensive tablecloth paper or tracing paper.

Designing tool, such as flexible curve or curved ruler; straightedge.

Decorator fabric.

Lightweight decorator fabric in accent color or coordinating print, for lining.

Heavy paper, for pressing pleats.

Mounting board, cut to length as determined on page 19.

Angle irons with flat-head screws; length of angle iron should be more than one-half the projection of board.

8 × 2½" (6.5 cm) flat-head screws for installing valance into wall studs; or molly bolts or toggle anchors for installing into drywall or plaster.

Staple gun and staples.

The gentle angle of the lower edge adds interest to the knife-pleated valance above. Dramatic curves and deep box pleats (opposite) create a tastefully elegant valance.

How to Make a Pattern for the Valance

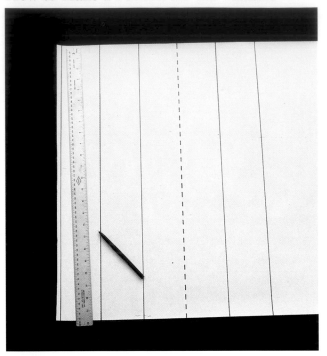

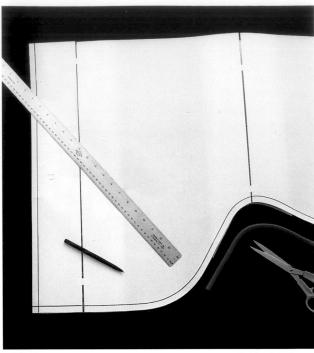

1) Follow step 1 on page 58. Unroll wide paper; cut paper with length equal to desired finished length of valance at long point plus 2" (5 cm). Mark the paper as in step 2 on page 58, running lines entire length of paper.

2) Follow step 3 on page 58. Draw shaped seamline of lower edge on folded pattern, following graphed sketch, with longest point ½" (1.3 cm) above cut edge of paper. Draw curved lines, using designing tool such as flexible curve or curved ruler; draw angled lines, using straightedge. Add ½" (1.3 cm) seam allowance below seamline. Cut out pattern.

Design Options for a Valance with a Shaped Lower Edge

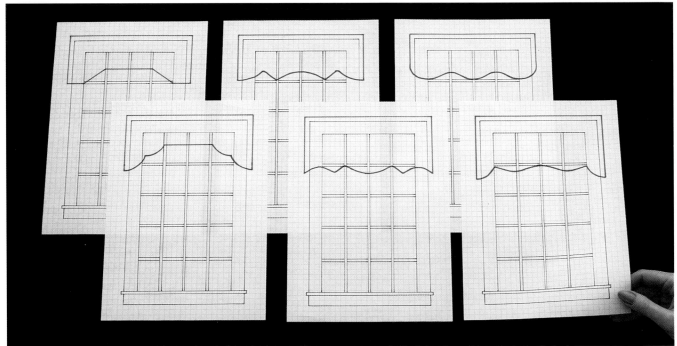

Design options for a valance with a shaped lower edge are limitless. Consider the style, number, and arrangement of pleats; structural features of the window itself; and the style of the undertreatment, if there is one. For best results, avoid severe angles and sharp curves. Follow the general measuring guidelines on page 11.

✂ Cutting Directions

Cut the valance fabric with the length equal to the desired finished length at the longest point plus 2" (5 cm).

Determine the approximate cut width by measuring the total width of the pattern, opposite; allow excess width for placing seams in folds of pleats. Cut the valance fabric to the necessary width, as in step 1 on page 59.

Cut the lining with the same length and width as the valance fabric.

How to Sew a Pleated Valance with a Shaped Lower Edge

1) **Follow** step 1 on page 59. Place valance fabric and lining right sides together; pin pattern in place, aligning upper and side edges. Cut valance fabric and lining along lower edge of pattern.

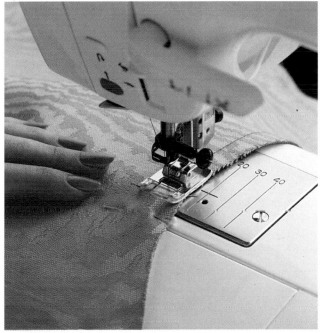

2) **Remove** pattern. Pin valance and lining together along lower and side edges; stitch ½" (1.3 cm) seam.

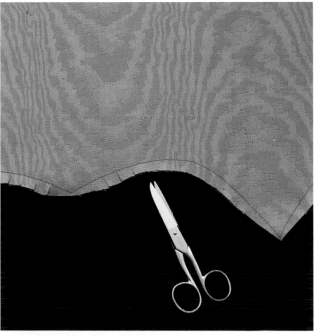

3) **Trim** outer corners, clip into inner corners, and clip seam allowances on curves. Complete valance as on pages 60 and 61, steps 3 to 8.

Awning Valances with Shaped Lower Edges

Use this versatile awning valance to give your kitchen, porch, or dining area the look often found in a bistro or outdoor cafe. In a child's bedroom, this window treatment can be used to create a playful circus atmosphere.

The main body of the awning is constructed from one or more fabric widths, with separate pieces for the rod pockets. Although the length of the awning may vary, a suitable length for most windows is 15" to 17" (38 to 43 cm). About 4" to 6" (10 to 15 cm) of this amount becomes the drop length. The lower edge of the valance can be shaped as desired in a repeating or symmetrical pattern, allowing for 8" (20.5 cm) returns on the outer edges. The awning valance is self-lined or lined in a coordinating fabric that will peek out frequently at the lower edge. For added interest, attach tassels, beads, or charms to the shaped lower edge.

The awning is supported by two curtain rods of equal length. If the awning is used between wall cabinets, a pressure rod is used for the upper rod. Otherwise, a

small-diameter cafe rod is mounted with cup hooks instead of the usual brackets. A canopy rod with an 8" (20.5 cm) projection is used, to hold the awning away from the window at the bottom.

✂ Cutting Directions

Make the awning pattern as on pages 68 and 69, steps 1 to 5; cut one awning piece from the outer fabric and one from the lining. For the upper rod pocket, cut a strip of the outer fabric, with the length of the strip 2" (5 cm) longer than the length of the rod and the width equal to twice the rod-pocket depth (page 11) plus 1" (2.5 cm) for seam allowances. For the lower rod pocket, cut a strip of the lining fabric 2" (5 cm) wide, with the length equal to the width of the awning pattern at the drop line.

YOU WILL NEED

Decorator fabric, for valance and lining.

Cafe rod with 3/8" to 7/16" (1 to 1.2 cm) diameter, 1" (2.5 cm) cup hooks, and plastic anchors sized for #4 screws, for upper rod if awning is not mounted between wall cabinets. Or pressure rod, for upper rod if awning is mounted between wall cabinets.

Canopy rod with 8" (20.5 cm) projection, #4 screws, and plastic anchors sized for #4 screws, for lower rod.

Drill and 5/32" drill bit.

Tassels, beads, or charms, for embellishment, optional.

How to Mount the Rods for an Awning Valance

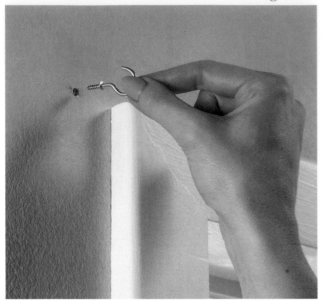

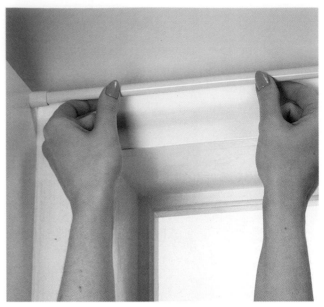

Cafe rod. Mark position for cup hooks about 1" (2.5 cm) outside and above window frame. Unless at wall stud, drill holes for plastic anchors, using 5/32" drill bit. Tap plastic anchors into drilled holes; screw cup hooks into anchors. Repeat to install cup hooks at 36" (91.5 cm) intervals. Hang cafe rod on cup hooks. Lower rod is mounted after awning is sewn.

Pressure rod. Mount a pressure rod between cabinets at top of window, following manufacturer's directions. Lower rod is mounted after awning is sewn.

How to Make the Pattern for an Awning Valance

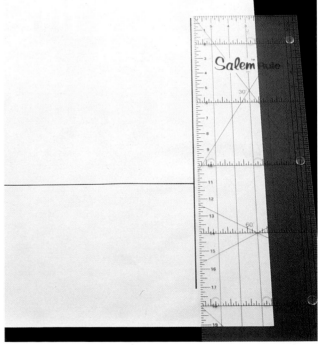

1) Measure the distance between outer cup hooks or distance between wall cabinets; this is the rod length measurement. On paper, draw a horizontal line equal to the rod length plus 16" (40.5 cm); this line marks the upper edge of the drop length and the lower rod pocket.

2) Draw perpendicular line at each end of horizontal line, extending 11" (28 cm) above the line and 6" (15 cm) below the line, for sides of valance.

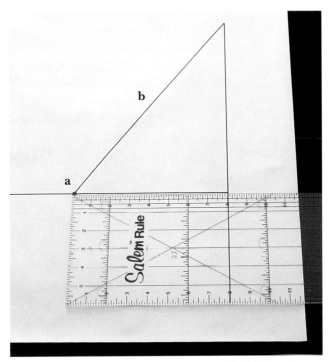

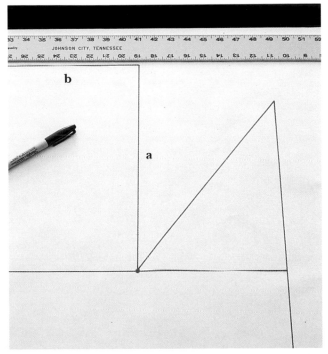

3) Mark a dot **(a)** on horizontal line 8" (20.5 cm) from each side; this marks point of dart. Draw line **(b)** from marked dot to upper end of vertical line for side of valance; repeat for other side. Measure length of diagonal line.

4) Draw vertical lines **(a)** of same length as diagonal lines, starting at marked dots. Draw horizontal line **(b)** across top of valance; this should measure same distance as upper rod length.

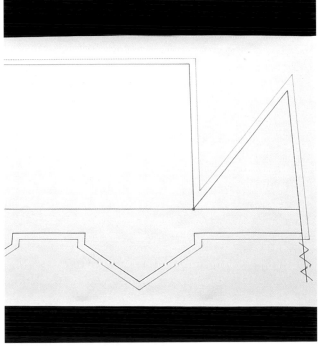

5) Draw design for the lower edge of valance, using symmetrical or repeating pattern; plan 8" (20.5 cm) of pattern on outer edges for returns. Shortest point of design should fall no less than 2" (5 cm) below line for drop length. Add ½" (1.3 cm) seam allowances on all sides.

6) Cut one awning piece from outer fabric and one from lining, piecing the fabric widths as necessary. Transfer line for drop length to right side of lining. Transfer markings for dart points to wrong sides of outer fabric and lining.

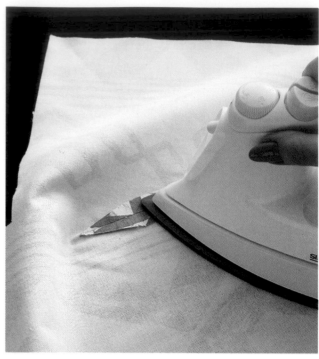

1) Press ¼" (6 mm) to wrong side on both long edges of lining strip for lower rod pocket. Turn under ½" (1.3 cm) twice at ends; stitch. Pin strip to lining, with top of strip along marked line for drop length and ends of strip 1" (2.5 cm) from side edges. Stitch close to top and bottom of strip.

2) Stitch darts in outer fabric, ½" (1.3 cm) from raw edges, stitching to marked dots. Clip to point of each dart; press the darts open. Repeat for darts in lining.

3) Press 1" (2.5 cm) to wrong side at each end of fabric strip for rod pocket; topstitch in place. Fold fabric strip in half lengthwise, wrong sides together; baste raw edges together.

4) Pin the rod pocket to upper edge of awning piece from outer fabric, with the ends of rod pocket at the dart seamlines and raw edges aligned. Stitch ½" (1.3 cm) seam.

5) Pin outer fabric and lining right sides together; stitch ½" (1.3 cm) seam around all edges, leaving 5" (12.5 cm) opening along side, for turning. Trim seam allowances along the shaped lower edge to ¼" (6 mm).

6) Clip to stitching line along any curves and inside corners. Trim diagonally across outside corners. Press lining seam allowances toward lining.

7) Turn awning right side out; press seamline of rod pocket and edges of awning. Slipstitch opening closed. Fold and press awning along dart seamlines, right side out. Embellish lower edge with beads, charms, or tassels as desired.

8) Insert rods into rod pockets. Hang awning from upper rod. Mark bracket positions for lower rod, directly under cup hooks or ends of pressure rod. Install lower rod.

Mock Cornices

Top treatments that resemble cornices can be made without carpentry or upholstery techniques. Mock cornices are mounted on flat curtain rods that measure 4½" (11.5 cm) wide. Fusible fleece applied inside the rod pocket gives the treatment a padded look. The top and bottom of the rod pocket are accented with fabric-covered welting or twisted welting. For added flair, a pleated or gathered skirt is sewn below the rod pocket.

These versatile top treatments can be used to dress up windows that have existing treatments, such as vertical or horizontal blinds, pleated shades, or curtains. In some cases, they may provide a totally new look, using existing wide flat rods.

For best results, select a lightweight fabric that can be successfully railroaded (page 12). This will eliminate the need for seams in the rod pocket. The skirt can be seamed in the center, hiding the seam in a pleat or gathers. Two skirt lengths and both rod-pocket pieces can be cut from one width of 54" (137 cm) decorator fabric, provided the skirt length does not exceed 16" (40.5 cm).

✂ Cutting Directions

Determine the desired finished width of the valance, the depth of the returns, and the desired finished length of the skirt. Preshrink decorator fabric and lining by steaming.

Cut a strip of decorator fabric for the front of the rod pocket, 6" (15 cm) wide, with the length equal to the desired finished width of the valance, including returns, plus 1" (2.5 cm) for end seams plus ½" (1.3 cm) for ease. Cut a strip of decorator fabric for the back of the rod pocket, 6" (15 cm) wide, with the length equal to the cut length of the front rod-pocket strip plus 1" (2.5 cm). Cut a strip of lining fabric for the front rod-pocket facing, with the same length and width as the front rod-pocket strip.

Cut decorator fabric for the skirt, with the length equal to the desired finished length plus 4½" (11.5 cm). If making a gathered skirt, the cut width of the skirt is equal to twice the desired finished width, including returns, plus 1" (2.5 cm). If making a pleated skirt, determine the cut width by making a pattern as on page 58, steps 1 to 3. Cut lining for the skirt, with the length equal to the finished length of the skirt plus ½" (1.3 cm) and the cut width equal to the cut width of the decorator fabric.

Cut bias fabric strips, if making fabric-covered welting, as on page 111, step 1.

Cut a strip of fusible fleece, 5" (12.5 cm) wide, with the length equal to the finished width of the valance, including returns, plus ½" (1.3 cm) for ease.

YOU WILL NEED

Decorator fabric.

Lining fabric.

Fusible fleece.

Fabric-covered welting, twisted welting, or 5/32" **(3.8 mm) cord and fabric,** for making fabric-covered welting.

Flat curtain rod, 4½" (11.5 cm) wide, with adjustable mounting brackets to obtain necessary projection.

Self-adhesive hook and loop tape.

Mock cornice with a gathered skirt (opposite) has a soft, relaxed look. Knife-pleated skirt and twisted welting create a crisp, tailored mock cornice (above).

1) Center fusible fleece strip on the wrong side of the front rod-pocket strip; fuse in place, following manufacturer's instructions.

2) Make fabric-covered welting (page 111) and attach it to upper and lower edges of front rod-pocket strip, if desired; begin and end welting ½" (1.3 cm) from ends of strip. Or attach purchased welting (page 113).

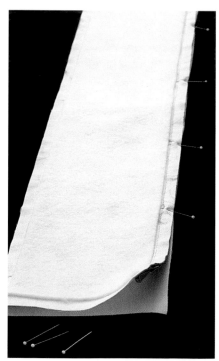

3) Place front rod pocket over the front rod-pocket facing strip, right sides together, aligning edges; pin along lower edge and ends.

4) Stitch ½" (1.3 cm) seam along lower edge and ends, using zipper foot and stitching with facing side down. Crowd cording by stitching just inside previous stitches.

5) Clip lower corners diagonally; turn front rod pocket right side out, and press. Baste upper edges together within ½" (1.3 cm) seam allowance.

6) Seam fabric for skirt, if necessary; repeat for skirt lining. Pin skirt and lining, right sides together, along lower edge. Stitch 2" (5 cm) from raw edges.

7) Press 2" (5 cm) hem allowance away from lining. Pin skirt to lining, right sides together, along sides, aligning upper edges; skirt will form fold even with lower edge of hem allowance. Stitch ½" (1.3 cm) side seams.

8) Clip lower corners diagonally. Press the lining side seam allowances toward lining. Turn skirt right side out, realigning upper edges; press. Baste the upper edges together.

9) Zigzag over a cord on right side of skirt within ½" (1.3 cm) seam allowance of upper edge.

(Continued on next page)

10) Divide skirt into eighths; pin-mark. Divide lower edge of back rod pocket into eighths, beginning and ending 1" (2.5 cm) from ends. Pin wrong side of skirt to right side of back rod pocket along lower edge, matching pin marks and raw edges.

11) Pull gathering cord on skirt to fit lower edge of back rod pocket; pin in place. Stitch ½" (1.3 cm) from raw edges. Press seam allowances toward back rod pocket.

12) Pin back rod pocket to front rod pocket along upper edge, right sides together; ends of back rod pocket extend 1" (2.5 cm) beyond ends of front rod pocket. With the front rod pocket on top, stitch ½" (1.3 cm) seam, using zipper foot; crowd cording.

13) Press seam allowances toward back rod pocket. Turn under ends of back rod-pocket strip ½" (1.3 cm) twice, encasing ends of seam allowances; stitch.

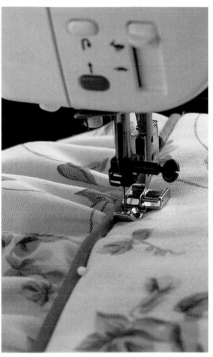

14) Turn skirt and back rod pocket down behind rod pocket. From the right side, pin skirt in place along the seamline at lower edge of rod pocket, just above welting.

15) Stitch in the ditch from the right side by stitching in the well of the seam above the welting, using a zipper foot.

16) Insert the curtain rod into rod pocket. Mount rod on bracket. Pull taut toward returns; secure returns to the sides of brackets, using self-adhesive hook and loop tape.

How to Sew a Mock Cornice with a Pleated Skirt

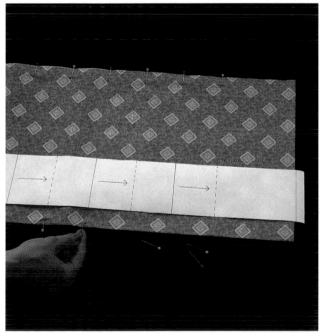

1) Make a pattern for the pleated skirt, as on page 58, steps 1 to 3. Follow steps 1 to 8 on pages 74 and 75. Lay the skirt faceup on flat surface; lay pattern over upper edge of skirt, aligning the marked seamlines to seamed outer edges. Transfer pattern markings to skirt. Repeat along lower edge.

2) Pin pleats in place along upper and lower edges of skirt; press. Baste along upper edge. Pin wrong side of skirt to right side of back rod pocket along lower edge; stitch. Press seam allowances toward the rod pocket. Complete mock cornice, following steps 12 to 16, opposite and above.

Curtains

Scalloped Curtains

For an interesting effect, the upper edge of curtain panels can be scalloped. This design detail works for stationary curtain panels that are attached to a rod by tabs or by clip-on or sew-on rings. Curtains attached by rings can also be made to traverse the rod and cover the window when necessary. Scalloped curtains may be lined or unlined, in any desired length. The hem may fall to a casual length just ½" (1.3 cm) below the window frame, to a more formal length ½" (1.3 cm) above the floor, or break at the floor with 2" (5 cm) of extra length. The scalloped edge is finished with a facing, using the same fabric as the curtain or a coordinating fabric.

Select mediumweight fabric with enough body to hold the shape of the scallop. If a print is selected, check to see that light from the window will not cause the facing to shadow through to the right side of the curtain.

For best results, the curtain should be made with returns on the outer edges to block side light. A tab or ring is positioned at the outer front corner, and the return is attached to the wall. For curtains with two panels that meet in the center, both panels should end with a tab or ring at the center edge.

When more than one width of fabric is used in a curtain panel, the scallop widths vary slightly from one fabric width to the next. This is done to avoid placing tabs or rings directly over a seam, making the seam highly visible. A seam is least visible if it is positioned 3" (7.5 cm) to the outside of the nearest tab or ring. This may result in scallop widths in the center of the panel being slightly narrower than the remaining scallops. Scallop depths are all equal, however, and fullness can be distributed so that tabs or rings are spaced evenly along the rod, making the difference in scallop width unnoticeable in the finished treatment.

Before mounting the rod above the window, consider the distance any rings or clips hang below the rod, as this will determine the highest point of the upper edge of the curtain. If making tab curtains, wrap a cloth tape measure over the rod to determine the desired length of the tab. Also determine the depth of the scallops. Shallow scallops of 2½" to 3" (6.5 to 7.5 cm) are appropriate for cafe curtains on a small window, whereas deep 8" (20.5 cm) scallops create a dramatic effect on floor-length curtains. Depending on how high the rod is mounted and the depth of the scallops, part of the upper window frame and even the glass may be exposed by the scallops.

Deep scallops and a breaking hem exaggerate the length of elegant jacquard curtains (opposite). Scalloped cafe curtains in a fresh, flowery print (above) capture the carefree mood of a breakfast nook.

✄ Cutting Directions

Mount the rod in the desired location above the window. Determine the finished length of the curtain by measuring from the clip, ring, or desired distance below the rod for tabs to where you want the lower edge of the curtain. The cut length of the decorator fabric is equal to the finished length of the curtain plus 8" (20.5 cm) for the bottom hem plus ½" (1.3 cm) for the seam allowance at the upper edge.

Determine the desired finished width of the curtain. The finished width of traversing curtains with rings is determined by measuring the length of the rod plus returns. The finished width of stationary panels is determined only by the space they cover plus returns. Multiply this amount by two times fullness. Divide this amount by the fabric width and round up or down to the nearest whole or half width, to determine the number of fabric widths needed. If the curtain is to be split between two panels, use only full and half widths in each panel.

Cut fabric for the facing, with the length equal to the scallop depth plus 4" (10 cm) and the width equal to the cut width of the curtain fabric.

The cut length of the lining is equal to the cut length of the decorator fabric minus the scallop depth minus 8" (20.5 cm).

If making tab curtains, cut a 3" (7.5 cm) strip of fabric for each tab, 1" (2.5 cm) longer than the desired finished length. You will need five tabs for the first full width plus four tabs for each additional full width and two tabs for each additional half width in each curtain panel.

Cut paper for the pattern, 2" (5 cm) longer than the desired scallop depth and 6" (15 cm) narrower than the seamed width of the curtain panel. This will be the finished width after hemming.

YOU WILL NEED

Decorator rod; clip-on rings or sew-on rings, if desired.

Decorator fabric, 48" to 54" (122 to 137 cm) wide, for curtains.

Matching or contrasting fabric, for facing.

Matching or contrasting fabric, for tabs, if desired.

Lining fabric, optional.

Paper, pencil, string, for making scallop pattern.

Drapery weights.

Pin-on rings and cup hooks or tenter hooks, for securing returns to wall.

How to Sew Unlined Scalloped Curtains

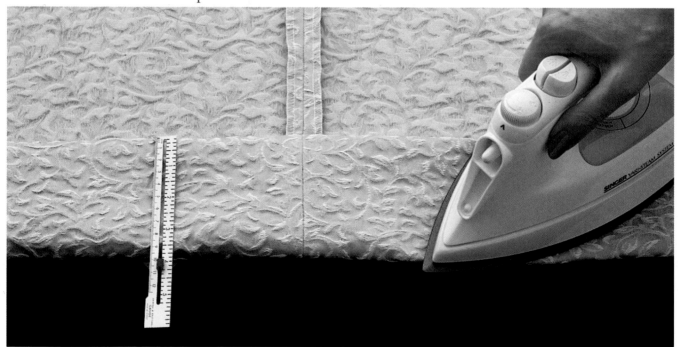

1) Seam fabric widths together as necessary for each curtain panel, adding any half widths at the return ends of the panels. Repeat for facings. At lower edge of curtain panel, press under 4" (10 cm) twice to wrong side; stitch to make double-fold hem, using blindstitch or straight stitch.

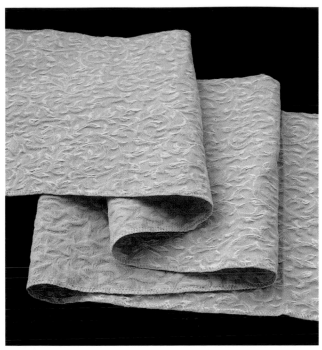

2) Finish the lower edge of the facing, using overlock, or turn under ¼" (6 mm) twice and stitch, using straight stitch.

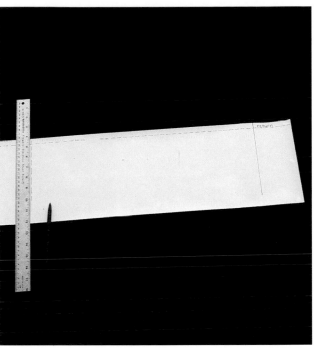

3) Mark ½" (1.3 cm) seam allowance across upper edge of pattern. Mark depth of return on one end of pattern; mark seam positions.

4) Mark point on upper seamline ½" (1.3 cm) away from return. Mark a point 3" (7.5 cm) beyond first seam from return.

5) Fold paper to divide space between marks into four equal parts if space represents whole width, or into two equal parts if space represents half width; crease to mark. Unfold.

(Continued on next page)

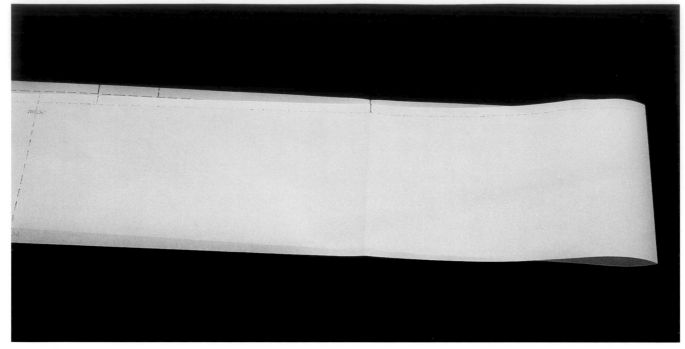

6) Divide any additional whole widths, falling between return end and opposite end of panel, into four equal parts, placing marks for tabs or rings nearest seams 3" (7.5 cm) beyond seams.

7) Mark point ½" (1.3 cm) from end; divide end width into four equal parts.

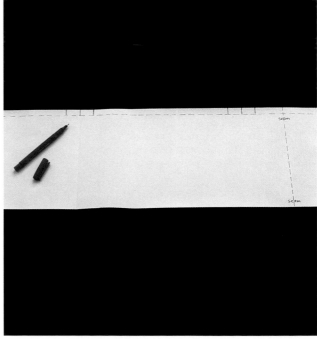

8) Mark scallop end points on the upper seamline, 1" (2.5 cm) on each side of the marks. This allows for ½" (1.3 cm) seam allowances in the scalloped edge and 1" (2.5 cm) space for tabs or rings.

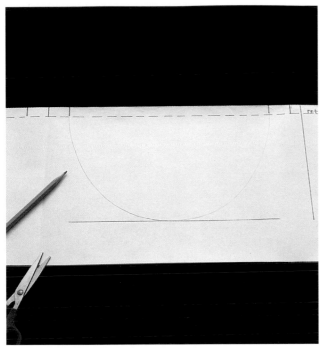

9) Mark depth of scallop in first space from return, measuring from upper edge of pattern; draw scallop from end points through depth mark. Refold, and cut first set of scallops.

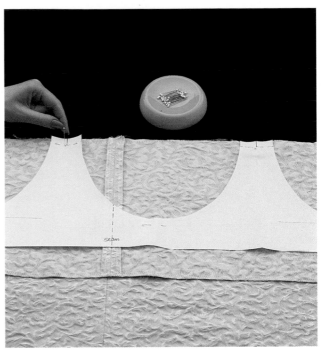

10) Repeat step 9 for each set of scallops. Place the facing over the curtain panel, right sides together, matching upper and side edges. Pin pattern over facing, aligning upper edges and seam marks; cut scallops. Transfer mark for return. For curtains without tabs, omit steps 11 to 13.

11) Fold each tab in half lengthwise, right sides together. Stitch ½" (1.3 cm) seam along cut edge; sew from one tab to the next, using continuous stitching.

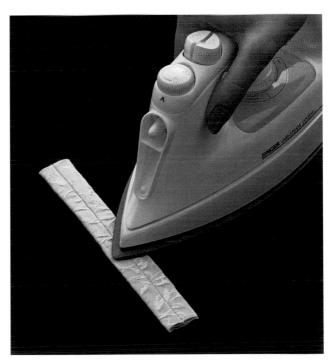

12) Turn tabs right side out. Center seam in back of each tab; press.

(Continued on next page)

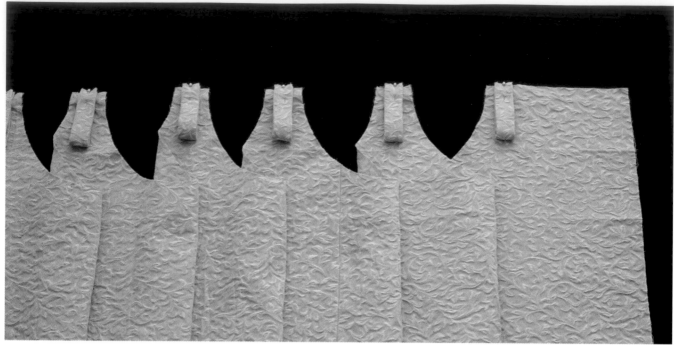

13) Fold each tab in half, aligning raw edges. Pin or baste tabs in place on right side of curtain, aligning raw edges of tabs to the upper edge of curtain and centering tabs between scallops. Pin tab at the return end with outer edges on return mark. Pin tab at the opposite end 3" (7.5 cm) from side of panel.

14) Pin facing to upper edge of curtain, right sides together, aligning raw edges. Stitch ½" (1.3 cm) seam. Zipper foot may be used to stitch close to tab. Trim seam; clip curves. Turn right side out, aligning outer raw edges; press.

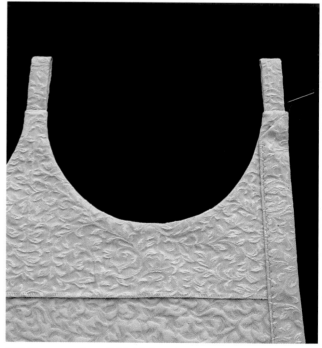

15) Press under 1½" (3.8 cm) twice on sides, folding facing and curtain panel as one fabric. Tack drapery weights inside the side hems, about 3" (7.5 cm) from lower edges. Stitch to make double-fold side hems, using blindstitch or straight stitch. Fold hem under diagonally at upper corner, if necessary; hand-stitch.

16) Hang curtain from the rod, using tabs or clip-on or sew-on rings. Attach pin-on ring to the inner edge of return, and secure to a tenter hook or cup hook in wall.

17) Space tabs or rings evenly on the rod as desired. Train the curtain so fabric in scallops rolls toward window; fabric at tabs or rings rolls outward, forming soft folds.

How to Sew Lined Scalloped Curtains

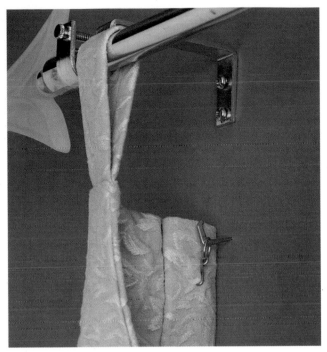

1) Follow step 1 on page 82. Seam lining widths together. Press under 2" (5 cm) twice at lower edge of lining; stitch to make double-fold hem. Pin facing to upper edge of lining, right sides together; stitch ½" (1.3 cm) seam. Press toward facing.

2) Follow steps 3 to 14 on pages 83 to 86. Align outer edges of facing and lining to outer edges of curtain. Lining will be 1" (2.5 cm) shorter than curtain panel. Complete curtain, following steps 15 to 17, folding lining and curtain panel as one fabric.

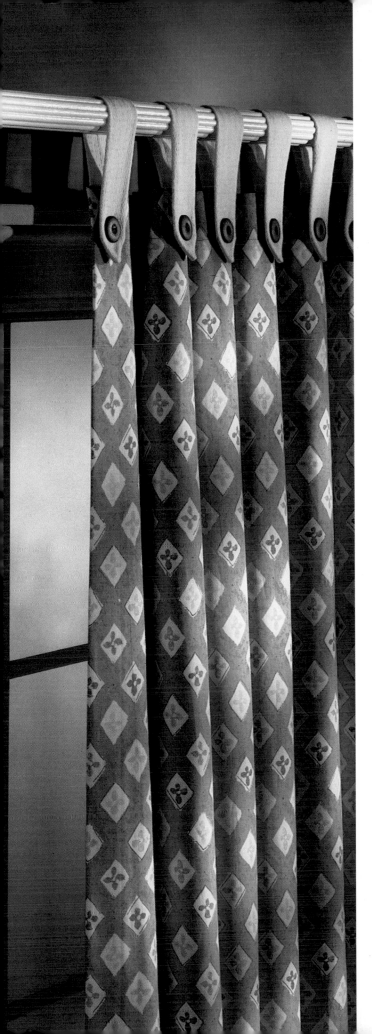

Button-tab Curtains

The unique design detail of these curtains draws attention to the upper edge. The curtain is suspended from a decorative pole by buttoned tabs. To avoid strain on the buttons, the tabs are sewn in place and the buttons are merely decorative.

Tab curtains are not intended to be opened and closed repeatedly, like a traverse drapery. The friction would cause unnecessary strain on the tabs. Therefore, this curtain style is generally made into two stationary panels at the sides of the window.

Button-tab curtains can be lined or unlined, depending on the fabric selection and the degree of light control and privacy required.

✂ Cutting Directions

Mount the rod in the desired location above the window as determined on page 90, steps 1 and 2. Determine the finished length of the curtain by measuring from 1" (2.5 cm) above the window frame to where you want the lower edge of the curtain. The cut length of the decorator fabric is equal to the finished length of the curtain plus 8" (20.5 cm) for the bottom hem plus ½" (1.3 cm) for the seam allowance at the upper edge.

Determine the desired finished width of each stationary curtain panel plus return. Multiply this amount by two times fullness. Divide this amount by the fabric width and round up or down to the nearest whole or half width, to determine the number of fabric widths needed.

Cut fabric for the facing 3" (7.5 cm) long, with the width equal to the cut width of the curtain fabric.

Cut a strip of fabric for each tab, 4½" (11.5 cm) wide, with the length as determined in step 1 on page 90. You will need five tabs for the first full width plus four tabs for each additional full width plus two tabs for each additional half width in each curtain panel.

Cut lining, if desired, with the length equal to the cut length of the curtain fabric minus 7" (18 cm) and the width equal to the cut width of the curtain fabric.

YOU WILL NEED

Decorator rod.

Decorator fabric, 48" to **54"** (122 to 137 cm) wide, for curtains and tabs.

Lining fabric, optional.

Drapery weights.

Buttons, ¾" to 1" (2 to 2.5 cm) wide; one for each tab.

Self-adhesive hook and loop tape, for securing returns to decorative brackets.

Pin-on rings and cup hooks or tenter hooks, for securing returns to wall.

How to Determine the Tab Length and Rod Placement

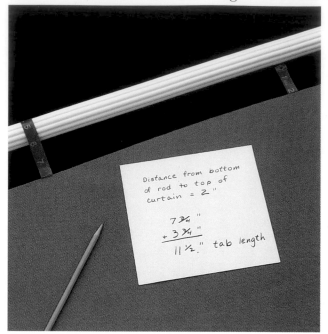

Distance from bottom
of rod to top of
curtain = 2"

7¾"
+ 3¾"
11½" tab length

1) Determine the tab length by wrapping a cloth tape measure over the rod the desired distance to top of curtain. Add 3¾" (9.5 cm) for tab extension and seam allowances. Measure distance from underside of rod to top of curtain.

2) Mount the rod a distance above window equal to this distance plus 1" (2.5 cm). This ensures that the window frame will not show above curtain.

How to Sew Unlined Button-tab Curtains

1) Seam fabric widths together as necessary for each curtain panel, adding any half widths at the return ends of the panels. Repeat for facing. At lower edge of curtain panel, press under 4" (10 cm) twice to wrong side; stitch to make double-fold hem, using blindstitch or straight stitch.

2) Fold each tab in half lengthwise, right sides together. Stitch ½" (1.3 cm) seam along cut edge; sew from one tab to the next, using continuous stitching.

3) Center the seam in back of tab; press, avoiding sharp creases on the outer edges. Mark a point ¼" (6 mm) from lower edge on seam; mark points 1¼" (3.2 cm) from the lower edge on outer folds.

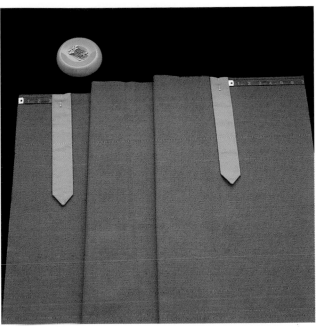

4) Sew from mark on outer fold to mark on seam; pivot, and stitch to mark on opposite fold, forming point of tab. Trim seam to ¼" (6 mm). Turn tab right side out; press.

5) Repeat steps 3 and 4 for all tabs. Pin a tab to top front of curtain, right side up, with outer edge of tab 3" (7.5 cm) from side of panel opposite the return; align raw edges. Pin another tab to top of curtain, with outer edge of tab a distance from return side equal to return depth plus 3" (7.5 cm).

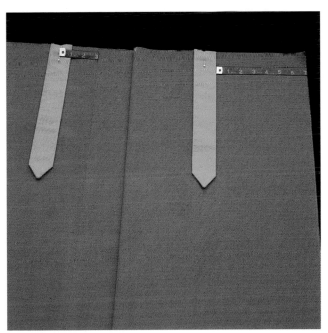

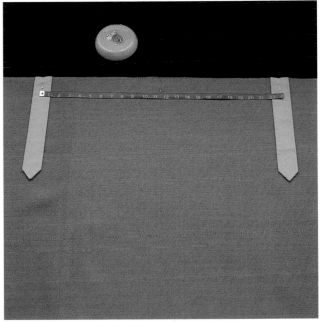

6) Center a tab 3" (7.5 cm) beyond first seam from return; pin. Repeat at any additional seams.

7) Measure distance between center of tab at return and center of tab beyond first seam from return. Divide distance by four for full fabric width or by two for half width; mark.

(Continued on next page)

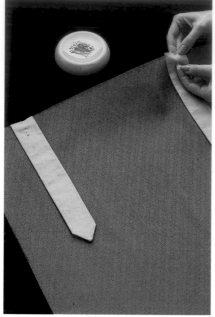

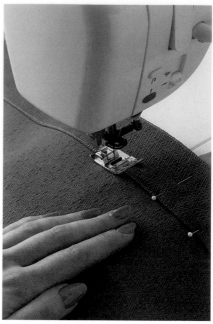

8) Repeat step 7 for each fabric width, measuring between tabs at seams. Center tabs at each mark; pin. Stitch all tabs in place within ½" (1.3 cm) seam allowance.

9) Press under ½" (1.3 cm) on one long edge of the facing. Pin facing to the curtain panel, right sides together, matching upper and side edges. Stitch ½" (1.3 cm) seam. Trim the facing seam allowance to ¼" (6 mm).

10) Press facing to wrong side of panel. Topstitch close to upper and lower edges of facing.

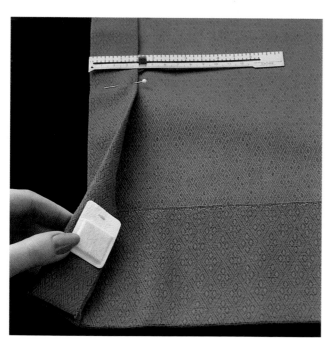

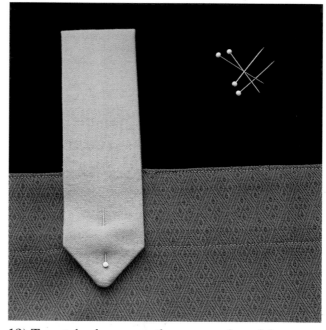

11) Align the outer raw edges of facing and curtain; press under 1½" (3.8 cm) twice on sides, folding facing and curtain as one fabric. Tack drapery weights inside the side hems, about 3" (7.5 cm) from lower edges. Stitch to make double-fold side hems, using blindstitch or straight stitch.

12) Turn tabs down over the upper edge of the curtain, aligning outer points of the tab to lower stitching line; pin.

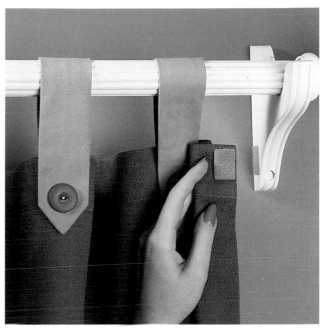

13) Tack tabs securely with sewing machine. Sew buttons over stitches.

14) Hang curtain from rod. Secure returns to inside of decorative bracket, using self-adhesive hook and loop tape. Or secure as on page 87, step 16. Space tabs evenly on rod as desired. Train curtain to fall in soft folds, with fabric at tabs rolling outward and fabric between tabs rolling toward window.

How to Sew Lined Button-tab Curtains

1) Follow step 1 at the bottom of page 90. Seam the lining widths together. Press under 2" (5 cm) twice at lower edge of lining; stitch to make double-fold hem.

2) Follow steps 2 to 8 on pages 90 to 92. Pin facing to upper edge of lining, right sides together; stitch ½" (1.3 cm) seam. Press the seam allowances toward facing. Follow steps 9 and 10 on page 92.

3) Align outer edges of facing and lining to outer edges of curtain. Lining will be 1" (2.5 cm) shorter than curtain panel. Complete the curtain, following steps 11 to 14, folding lining and curtain panel as one fabric.

Curtains with Attached Valances

Curtains with attached valances have a clean, updated look. Self-styling tape sewn at the top of the curtain gathers the upper edge in an attractive pattern. These stationary curtains can be made as two separate panels with attached valances, hanging at the sides of the window. Or, for another look, two panels that meet in the center and share an attached valance can be held back at the sides of the window with decorative hardware or tiebacks.

For best results, curtains with attached valances are made from lightweight fabric. The curtain panels may be lined, if desired. The valances can be made from either matching or coordinating fabric. The bottom of the valance is bound with a contrasting fabric, accenting the lower edge and eliminating the need for a hem.

Select a self-styling tape that will gather the upper edge in the desired pattern. Mount either style of treatment on a decorator rod with rings. Or, if desired, use a standard curtain rod to mount a treatment with two panels under one valance.

Two curtain panels share one continuous attached valance (opposite). The curtain top is gathered into even pencil pleats, using self-styling shirring tape. Smocking tape, used in the separate curtain panels above, gathers the upper edge into a unique design.

Types of Self-styling Tapes

Self-styling cords and hook loops are woven into the styling tapes to create several different looks. Shirring tape **(a)** draws curtain panels into narrow, evenly spaced pencil pleats. Smocking tape **(b)** creates soft, alternating pleats for a look that resembles smocking. Two rows of smocking tape can be applied for a more dramatic effect. Pleating tape **(c)** is used to create a classic pinch-pleated look. If using this tape, plan spacing so that pleats form at the front corner of the return edge and at least 2" (5 cm) from the inner edge.

✂ Cutting Directions

Determine the desired finished length of the curtain. If using a decorative rod with rings, measure from the pin holes in the rings to the desired length. If using a standard curtain rod, measure from the top of the rod to where you want the lower edge of the curtain; then add ½" (1.3 cm) so the curtain will extend above the rod. Determine the desired finished width of the curtain, including returns. Divide this amount by two for a curtain with two panels under one valance.

Cut fabric for the curtain panel with the cut length equal to the desired finished length plus 8½" (21.8 cm). The cut width of the fabric is equal to the finished width, including returns, multiplied by the desired fullness plus 6" (15 cm) for double-fold 1½" (3.8 cm) side hems. Fullness is determined by the self-styling tape; most tapes require two-and-one-half times fullness.

If lining is desired, cut lining fabric with the cut length equal to the cut length of the curtain fabric minus 5" (12.5 cm) and the cut width equal to the cut width of the curtain.

Cut fabric for the valance with the cut length equal to the desired finished length of the valance plus ½" (1.3 cm). For a single-panel curtain, the cut width of the valance is the same as the cut width of the curtain panel. For a two-panel curtain with one attached valance, the cut width of the valance is equal to the combined cut widths of the two panels minus 6" (15 cm).

Cut strips of fabric, 2" (5 cm) wide, to bind the lower edge of the valance. The length of the binding strip after seaming is equal to the cut width of the valance minus 5" (12.5 cm).

YOU WILL NEED

Decorator fabric, for curtain and valance.

Contrasting fabric, for binding the lower edge of the valance.

Drapery weights.

Self-styling tape.

Floss holder or small square of thin cardboard.

Decorator rod with rings; or standard curtain rod.

Drapery pins.

Pin-on rings and cup hooks or tenter hooks, for securing returns to wall.

Decorative holdbacks; or tieback holders and purchased tiebacks, for curtain with two panels that meet in the center and share an attached valance.

How to Sew a Curtain with an Attached Valance

1) **Seam** fabric widths together as necessary for the curtain panel. At lower edge of curtain panel, press under 4" (10 cm) twice to wrong side; stitch to make double-fold hem, using blindstitch or straight stitch. Repeat for lining, if desired, pressing under 2" (5 cm) twice. For unlined curtain, omit step 2.

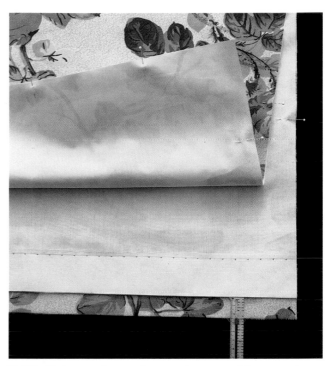

2) **Pin** lining and curtain panel wrong sides together, aligning the upper and side edges. Lower edge of the lining will be 1" (2.5 cm) above the lower edge of curtain. Baste along the upper edge within ½" (1.3 cm) seam allowance.

3) **Press** under 1½" (3.8 cm) twice on sides of the curtain; if lined, fold the lining and curtain as one fabric. Tack drapery weights inside the side hems, about 3" (7.5 cm) from lower edges. Stitch to make double-fold hems, using blindstitch or straight stitch.

4) **Seam** valance fabric widths together as necessary. Seam binding strips together with diagonal seams; trim to ¼" (6 mm). Press seams open. Press under ⅜" (1 cm) along one long edge.

(Continued on next page)

5) Stitch remaining edge of binding strip to lower edge of the valance, right sides together, stitching ½" (1.3 cm) from raw edges; begin and end binding strip 2½" (6.5 cm) from sides of valance. Press seam allowances toward binding.

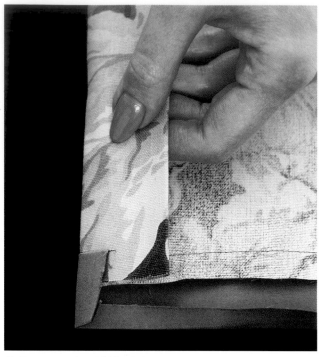

6) Press under 1½" (3.8 cm) twice on sides of the valance. Stitch to make double-fold hems, using blindstitch or straight stitch.

7) Turn binding strip over lower edge of valance, encasing raw edges. From right side of valance, pin binding in place along seamline, catching pressed edge of binding on wrong side.

8) Stitch in the ditch from the right side by stitching in the well of the seam.

9) Pin right side of valance to wrong side of curtain panel, matching upper raw edges. For curtain with two panels under one valance, butt inner edges of curtain panels. Stitch ½" (1.3 cm) seam; press open.

10) Fold the valance to front side of curtain along seamline; press.

11) Cut self-styling tape 3" (7.5 cm) longer than the width of curtain panel. Turn under 1½" (3.8 cm) on ends of tape, and use pin to pick out cords. Side of tape with hook loops is right side.

(Continued on next page)

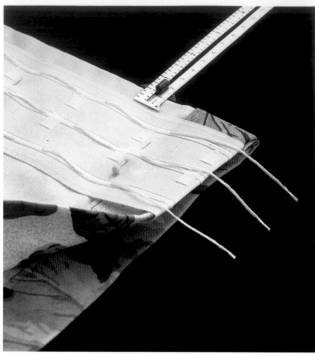

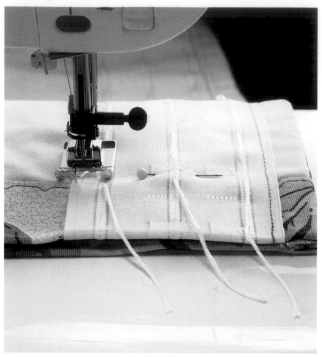

12) Lay curtain facedown on flat surface. Pin self-styling tape to curtain, with upper edge of tape ½" (1.3 cm) below upper edge of curtain; pin through curtain and valance. (Hook loops are at upper edge of tape.) Tuck turned-under ends of tape between curtain and valance.

13) Stitch along top and bottom edges of the tape; do not catch cords in stitching. For smocking tape, stitch again close to remaining cords.

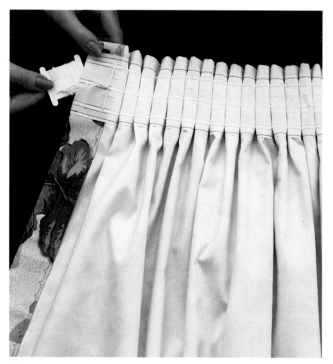

14) Secure the cords at both ends of tape, using one or two overhand knots to prevent cords from being pulled out. Pull cords at one end to gather curtain to finished width, as determined by the styling tape. Adjust fullness evenly.

15) Knot the cords securely at sides of curtain. Wind excess cord around floss holder or small square of thin cardboard; tuck into space between curtain and valance, or secure to back of curtain.

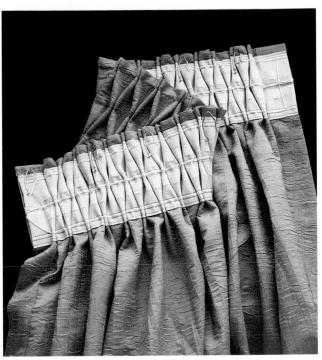

16) Standard curtain rod. Insert drapery pins at ends of the panel, with remaining pins evenly spaced, about 3" (7.5 cm) apart; tops of pins should be ½" (1.3 cm) from top of curtain.

16) Decorative rod. Insert drapery pins at inner ends of panels and at front corners of returns. Insert the remaining pins, evenly spaced, about 3" (7.5 cm) apart, with tops of pins ¼" (6 mm) from top of curtain.

17) Standard curtain rod. Hook drapery pins over the rod.

17) Decorative rod. Insert drapery pins into eyes of rings. Attach pin-on ring to inner edge of return, and secure to a cup hook or tenter hook in wall.

Curtains with Contrasting Cuffs

Curtains can be given added flair with contrasting cuffs. The heading, faced in a fabric to coordinate or contrast with the main curtain fabric, is made extra long so that it droops forward over the rod pocket. The curtains can be made as two rod-pocket panels that meet in the center and tie back, mounted on standard curtain rods or flat rods 2½" (6.5 cm) wide. If the window is very narrow, the curtain can be made as a single panel that ties back to one side. If preferred, a decorative rod can be used and the panels can hang separately at the sides of the window.

For a curtain with a more contemporary look, simply lengthen the heading and mount it with clip-on hooks to a decorative rod. The cuff then folds down completely over the top of the curtain, which hangs in soft, deep folds rather than gathers.

Lightweight to mediumweight fabrics can be used, depending on the look preferred. Curtains made from lightweight fabric can be interlined with flannel for a padded effect. This effect can be accentuated by adding 10" to 15" (25.5 to 38 cm) to the finished length, allowing them to billow out above the tiebacks and extend onto the floor at the hemline. Select flannel for the interlining that is wide enough to railroad, if possible, eliminating the need for seams. If seams are necessary, trim seam allowances to ¼" (6 mm), press the seams open, and flatten them with a running zigzag stitch.

✂ Cutting Directions

Determine the finished length of the curtain, including extra length for billowing, if desired. If using a decorative rod with rings and clip-on hooks, measure from the highest point inside the clip. If using a curtain rod, measure from the top of the rod to where you want the lower edge of the curtain.

Cut fabric for the curtain with the length equal to the finished length plus 8" (20.5 cm) for the hem plus ½" for the seam allowance at the top plus the depth of the cuff heading; allow 6" to 8" (15 to 20.5 cm) for the cuff heading.

The cut width of the fabric is equal to the desired finished width, including returns, multiplied by the desired fullness; allow two to two-and-one-half times fullness.

For rod-pocket curtains, cut fabric for the contrasting cuff with the length equal to the heading depth plus the rod-pocket depth (page 11) plus 1" (2.5 cm). For curtains that mount with clip-on hooks to a decorative rod, the cut length of the heading is equal to the heading depth plus 2½" (6.5 cm). The cut width of the heading is equal to the cut width of the curtain fabric minus 4" (10 cm).

Cut the lining fabric with the length equal to the cut length of the decorator fabric minus 5"

(12.5 cm) and the width equal to the cut width of the decorator fabric.

Cut interlining, if desired, with the cut length equal to the cut length of the lining minus 3½" (9 cm) and the cut width equal to the cut width of the lining minus 3" (7.5 cm).

YOU WILL NEED

Lightweight to mediumweight decorator fabric.

Contrasting decorator fabric, for cuff.

Drapery lining.

Flannel interlining, optional.

Drapery weights.

Standard curtain rod or flat rod, 2½" (6.5 cm) wide, for rod-pocket curtain that covers entire rod; or decorative rod or pole, for rod-pocket curtain with separate panels that hang at the sides of the window.

Decorative rod and rings with clip-on hooks, for contemporary-style curtain.

Decorative holdbacks; or tieback holders and purchased tiebacks, for tieback curtains.

Pin-on rings and cup hooks or tenter hooks, for securing returns of clip-on-ring-style curtain to wall.

How to Sew a Curtain with a Contrasting Cuff

1) Seam the fabric widths together as necessary for curtain panel. At lower edge of curtain panel, press under 4" (10 cm) twice to wrong side; stitch to make double-fold hem, using blindstitch or straight stitch. Repeat for lining, pressing under 2" (5 cm) twice. For curtain without interlining, omit steps 2 and 3.

2) Seam interlining widths, if necessary. Finish lower edge of interlining, using overlock stitch; or turn edge under ¼" (6 mm), and zigzag.

3) **Pin** interlining to wrong side of lining, aligning upper edges; side edges of interlining will be 1½" (3.8 cm) in from side edges of lining. Baste together scant ½" (1.3 cm) from raw edge of interlining on sides and upper edges.

4) **Pin** lining and curtain panel wrong sides together, aligning upper and side edges. Lower edge of lining will be 1" (2.5 cm) above lower edge of curtain; interlining, if used, will be encased between curtain and lining. Baste along the upper edge within ½" (1.3 cm) seam allowance.

5) **Press** under 1½" (3.8 cm) twice on sides of the curtain, folding the lining and curtain as one fabric. Tack drapery weights inside the side hems, about 3" (7.5 cm) from lower edge.

6) **Stitch** along inner fold to make double-fold hems, using blindstitch or straight stitch.

(Continued on next page)

7) **Seam** the cuff fabric widths as necessary. Press under ½" (1.3 cm) twice at sides; stitch. Press under ½" (1.3 cm) along one long edge.

8) **Pin** remaining edge of cuff to upper edge of the curtain, right sides together. Stitch ½" (1.3 cm) seam; press open.

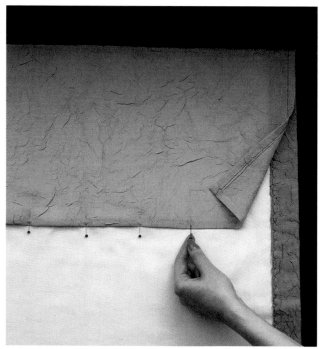

9) **Turn** cuff to back; press along seamline. Pin in place along lower folded edge.

10) **Stitch** along foldline. Stitch again a distance away from foldline equal to the rod-pocket depth for the rod-pocket style, or 1½" (3.8 cm) for clip-on-ring style. Hand-stitch ends of heading closed, if desired.

How to Install a Curtain with a Contrasting Cuff

Rod-pocket style. Insert rod into rod pocket; mount rod on brackets. Distribute fullness evenly. Arrange heading to fall forward over rod pocket, exposing contrasting cuff.

Tieback curtains. Fanfold curtain loosely at height of tieback, starting from inner edge and folding toward side. Secure with tieback or holdback. Billow curtain above tieback or holdback, if desired.

Clip-on-ring style. Fold cuff forward over front of the curtain along upper stitching line. Attach rings to the fold, placing outermost rings at depth of return from ends; place innermost rings at side hems. Space the remaining rings as desired, and arrange rings on rod, hiding curtain seams in folds between rings. Attach pin-on rings to inner edges of returns; secure to cup hooks or tenter hooks in wall.

Welting

Welting adds an attractive emphasis to the outer edge of a curtain panel or valance. Fabric-covered welting can be purchased in a limited selection of colors and sizes. For more variety, welting can be made by covering cording of the desired size with fabric to match or contrast with the window treatment fabric. If a more elegant look is desired, twisted welting can be purchased and sewn into outer seamed edges.

You may choose to add welting to the edge of a valance, such as the gathered pickup valance on page 50. The welting adds stiffness to the lower edge for a more defined shaping.

To make welting, fabric strips are cut on the bias, allowing for greater flexibility around curves and corners. The width of the bias strips can be determined by measuring the circumference of the cord and adding 1" (2.5 cm) for two ½" (1.3 cm) seam allowances.

Twisted welting, an ornate alternative to covered welting, is available in a variety of styles, colors, and sizes. A welt tape, or lip, is attached to decorative cord, for sewing into a seam. From the right side of the welting, the inner edge of the tape is not visible. For a more finished appearance, be sure to position the welting right side down on the right side of the decorative fabric.

How to Make and Attach Fabric-covered Welting

1) Fold fabric diagonally so selvage is parallel to crosswise grain; cut on the fold. Cut bias fabric strips of desired width, cutting ends of the strips at 45° angle on straight grain.

2) Seam the strips together as necessary; press the seams open. Cut end of strip straight across. Center the cording on wrong side of the fabric strip, with the end of the cording 1" (2.5 cm) from the end of the strip; fold end of strip over cording.

3) Fold the fabric strip around the cording, wrong sides together, matching raw edges and encasing end of cording.

(Continued on next page)

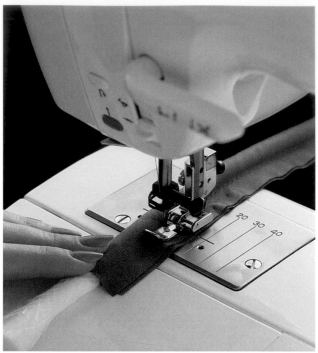

4) Machine-baste close to cording, using zipper foot, to create welting. Baste to end of cord.

5) Stitch welting to right side of curtain or valance, as indicated in project instructions, matching raw edges and stitching over previous stitches. Stop stitching 5" (12.5 cm) from desired end point for welting.

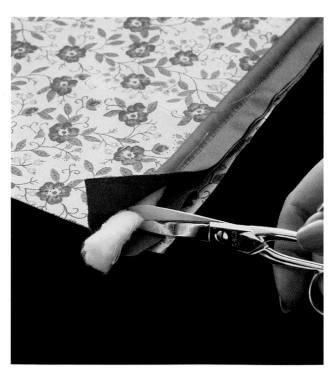

6) Cut welting 1" (2.5 cm) beyond desired end point. Remove stitching from end of welting, and cut the cording even with desired end point.

7) Fold end of fabric strip over cording, encasing end of the cording. Finish stitching welting to curtain or valance fabric.

How to Attach Twisted Welting

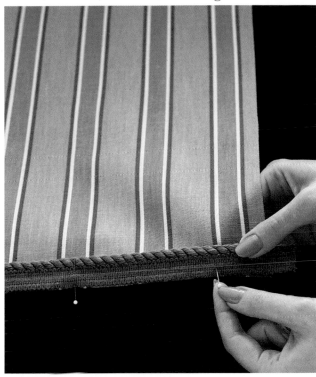

1) Pin the twisted welting to curtain or valance fabric, right sides together, with welt ½" (1.3 cm) from raw edge and the ends extending 1" (2.5 cm) beyond starting and stopping points.

2) Remove stitching from welting tape for about 1½" (3.8 cm) at ends.

3) Turn welting tape into seam allowance; pin or tape in place. Turn untwisted cords into the seam allowance, following pattern of welt and flattening them as much as possible; pin.

4) Stitch welting to fabric, ½" (1.3 cm) from raw edge, using zipper foot and crowding welting. Trim ends of welting.

Flat Bias Edging

Flat bias edging is an attractive accent detail that can be applied to the lower edge of lined valances or along the inner edge of banding strips on curtain panels. Usually sewn in a lightweight fabric of a contrasting color, flat bias edging adds a designer touch without the stiffness or bulk of fabric-covered welting.

The width of the flat bias edging may vary from ⅛" to ½" (3 mm to 1.3 cm), depending on the project and the desired appearance. Cut bias strips with a width equal to twice the desired finished width plus 1" (2.5 cm).

How to Make and Attach Flat Bias Edging

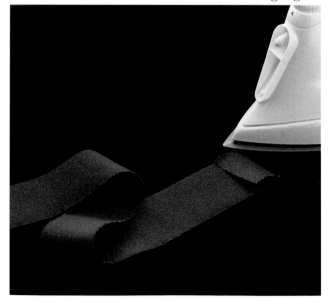

1) **Follow** step 1 on page 111. Seam strips together as necessary for desired length. Press seams open. Cut end of strip straight across. For edging with finished ends, fold back 1" (2.5 cm) at end of strip; press.

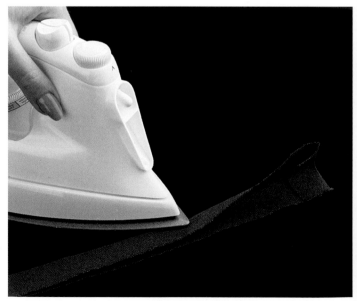

2) **Fold** strip in half lengthwise, wrong sides together; press. Take care not to stretch bias strip.

3) **Stitch** edging to right side of valance or banding, as indicated in project instructions, matching the raw edges. Check width measurement of edging often. Stop stitching 5" (12.5 cm) from desired end point, for edging with finished ends.

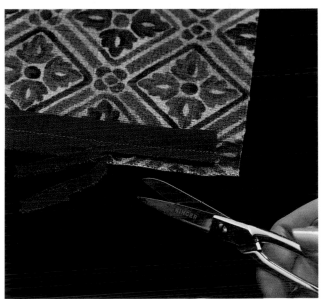

4) **Cut** the edging 1" (2.5 cm) beyond the desired end point, if finished end is desired. Fold back cut end 1" (2.5 cm), encasing the raw edge; press. Finish stitching edging to valance or banding. Trim edging seam allowance to ¼" (6 mm) to reduce bulk.

Fringe

The appearance of a window treatment can be changed dramatically, simply by adding fringe. Decorator fringes are available in a wide range of styles and colors, many with coordinating braids, tassels, or tiebacks. They may be made from synthetic or natural fibers, or a combination of fibers with interesting textural effects.

Many fringes have decorative headings and should be sewn on the outer surface of the window treatment. Some styles have a plain heading and are intended to be sewn into a seam, encasing the heading and exposing only the fringe.

Consider the length of the fringe when planning the window treatment. Though long fringes offer a dramatic look, they also severely affect the finished length of the treatment.

1) Brush fringe is a dense row of cotton, or a blend of cotton and synthetic, threads, all cut to the same length. When fringe is purchased, the cut edge is usually secured with a chain stitch, which should be left intact until the application is completed. After removing the chain stitch, fluff out the fringe by steaming and gentle brushing.

2) Cut fringe has a decorative heading and is similar to brush fringe, but usually not as dense. The cut threads of this fringe are often multicolored in a blend of fibers.

3) Loop fringe is made with a decorative heading. It is available in cotton, synthetic, or a combination of fibers. Just as the name implies, the fringe is composed of a series of overlapping looped threads. The loops may be all the same length or arranged in a pattern of varying lengths.

4) Tassel fringe is a continuous row of miniature tassels attached to a decorative heading. The tassels, often separated by loops, may be multicolored and multifibered.

5) Knot fringe is usually made of long cotton threads that are tied in single or multiple rows of knots just below the plain heading.

6) Ball fringe is a continuous row of pom-poms hanging from a plain heading. Though recognized as a casual craft fringe, some styles of ball fringe are more ornate and suitable for embellishing window treatments.

7) Bullion fringe is a continuous row of twisted cords attached to a decorative heading. Styles range from very heavy long fringe to lightweight short fringe with single-color or multicolored cords. Cotton bullion fringe is quite casual, while rayon or acetate bullion fringes can be used for very elegant applications.

Tips for Attaching Fringe

Decorative heading. 1) Apply liquid fray preventer liberally to area of heading that will be cut; allow to dry completely before cutting fringe.

2) Pin or glue-baste fringe in desired location on right side of finished window treatment, turning under ¾" (2 cm) at ends of heading. Straight-stitch along top and bottom of heading.

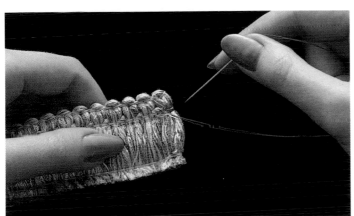

Plain heading. 1) Cut the fringe between the loops; hand-stitch cut ends to prevent raveling.

2) Machine-baste fringe to the right side of prepared window treatment panel, placing the fringe heading within the seam allowance. Pin panel and lining right sides together; stitch, encasing fringe heading.

Banding

Banding defines the edges of a curtain or shade. It can be used to accent one or two colors in the fabric or to repeat a color or print used elsewhere in the room.

Topstitched banding can be applied to lined or unlined treatments, preferably before hemming the sides and lower edge. This eliminates the need to sew through extra layers when applying the banding and does not alter the cut width or length of the fabric. For best results, plan carefully, taking all hem allowances into consideration when marking the banding placement lines. Topstitched banding, usually set in from the edges of the treatment, can be mitered at the corners, or the bands can cross each other and run into the side and lower hems.

Faced banding, applied to the outer edges of a window treatment, can eliminate the need for side or lower hems. It is suitable for treatments made from lightweight to sheer fabrics, offering stability around the outer edges as well as a decorative effect. If the treatment is banded both horizontally and vertically, mitered corners give it a finishing touch.

✂ Cutting Directions

Cut banding strips 1" (2.5 cm) wider than the desired finished width. Whenever possible, cut the strips from the lengthwise grain of the fabric, eliminating or minimizing the need for seams. For topstitched banding that runs into the side or lower hem, the length of the banding is equal to the cut length or width of the treatment. For treatments with mitered topstitched banding, determine the placement of the banding and add ½" (1.3 cm) to the length of each adjoining strip for each mitered corner.

For treatments with faced banding, the cut length or width of the treatment is determined by adding a ½" (1.3 cm) seam allowance for each banded edge to the finished length or width plus any other considerations, such as headings, rod pockets, or hems, for edges that are not banded.

How to Apply Topstitched Banding

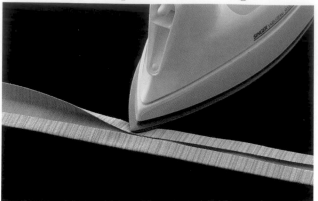

1) Press under ½" (1.3 cm) along both long edges of each banding strip. Omit steps 2 and 3 for bands without mitered corners.

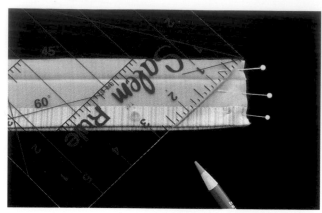

2) Unfold outer pressed edge at end. Mark a point ½" (1.3 cm) from end of strip on foldline. Pin ends of adjoining strips right sides together. Draw a line from marked point to pressed edge, at 45° angle.

3) Stitch along line to marked point; pivot, and stitch to edge at right angle from previous stitching line. Trim seam allowance to ¼" (6 mm); trim diagonally at pivot point. Press seam open; turn outer edge to back along pressed foldline.

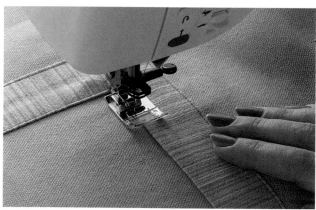

4) Repeat steps 2 and 3 for each mitered corner. Mark placement for banding on the treatment. Pin or glue-baste banding along marked lines. Topstitch in place close to pressed edges.

How to Apply Faced Banding

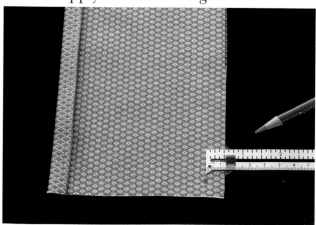

1) Press under ½" (1.3 cm) along one long edge of each banding strip. Repeat for all facing strips. Mark a point ½" (1.3 cm) from end of strip, ½" (1.3 cm) from unpressed edge. Repeat for all strips.

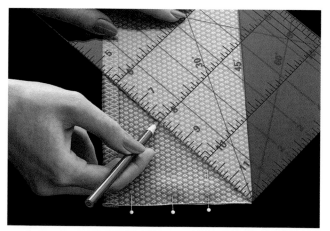

2) Pin ends of adjoining strips right sides together, matching pressed edges and raw edges. Draw a line from marked point to pressed edge, at 45° angle.

3) Stitch along line through marked point to outer corner. Trim seam allowance to ¼" (6 mm); press open. Repeat for each set of adjoining strips, mitering corners.

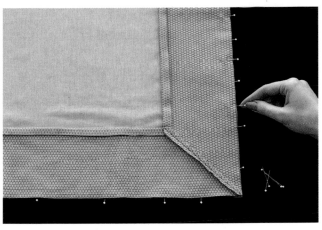

4) Pin banding strip faceup to right side of treatment, matching raw edges. Pin facing strip over banding strip, right sides together, matching raw edges and mitered seams.

5) Stitch ½" (1.3 cm) from raw edges through all layers; pivot stitching at mitered seams.

6) Trim the seam allowances diagonally across the corner. Fold out facing strip, and press seam open between band and facing, getting as close as possible to corners.

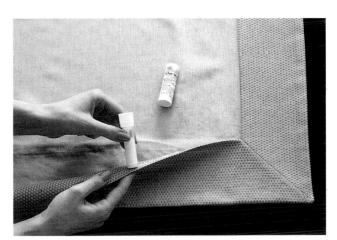

7) Turn the facing to back of treatment; press along seam. Glue-baste or pin banding and facing strips in place along inner pressed edges.

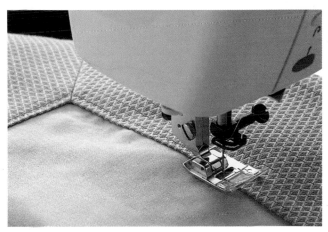

8) Topstitch along inner edge of band, catching inner edge of facing on back of treatment.

Drape narrow decorative cord along the upper edge of a scalloped curtain (page 81), echoing the arc of the scallops. Hand-tack cord at the base of each tab or ring.

Cords & Tassels

Decorative cord gives a window treatment the look of elegance and high style. It can be draped in creative ways to emphasize design lines of the treatment or used for opulent tiebacks. Tassels are the perfect accompaniments for cord embellishments, since they are designed to look like beautifully ravelled cord ends. By themselves, tassels can be used for decorative accents in various ways.

Decorative cords and tassels are available in a variety of colors and sizes as well as fiber contents. Some cords are made of decorative threads wrapped around a plain cotton core and then twisted into a rope. Other twisted rope styles are made entirely of decorative threads.

Purchased cord and tassel tiebacks, while impressive, can also be very expensive. Decorative cord can be purchased in precut lengths, called *chair ties*, with

attached tassels at the ends; however, the length is not adjustable. As an attractive alternative, cords that are made entirely of decorative threads can be successfully raveled and given self tassels. Cords that do not ravel attractively can be given fringe end caps.

YOU WILL NEED

For self tassel:

Decorative cord; about 12" (30.5 cm) extra cord is needed for each tassel.

Heavy thread.

Gimp or other narrow decorative braid in coordinating color; needle and thread to match gimp or braid.

For end cap:

Heavy thread.

Liquid fray preventer.

Fringe with decorative heading, in color and fiber content to coordinate with decorative cord.

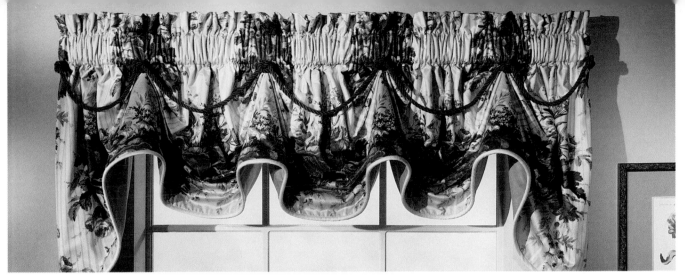

Drape decorative cord between the bells of a gathered pickup valance (page 50) to emphasize the curved lines of the swags. Select cord to match or coordinate with the welting at the lower edge. Tie a knot in the cord at the top of each bell, and hand-stitch it to the valance. Finish the ends of the cords with self tassels or end caps.

Glue decorative cord along the upper edge of a pleated valance (page 56), using hot glue. Hang matching tassels at outer front corners.

Attach tassels at the bottom of each row of rings on a butterfly Roman shade (page 31) for a more elegant look. Hand-tack lower folds together to support the weight of the tassels.

Secure tieback curtains with a length of decorative cord. Finish the cord ends with fringe end caps or self tassels.

1) **Bind** cord with heavy thread 3" to 4" (7.5 to 10 cm) from end. Ravel ends of cord up to knot; steam press to straighten threads.

2) **Cut** a length of cord 6" to 8" (15 to 20.5 cm) long. Ravel cord, keeping sets of threads separate; steam press to straighten threads.

3) **Layer** sets of thread on flat surface. Place raveled cord end over layered threads, aligning ends.

4) **Wrap** layered threads evenly around the cord. Bind the wrapped cord with heavy thread just above first binding.

5) Fold upper threads down over lower threads and raveled cord end, forming tassel. Bind with heavy thread ¾" (2 cm) below top of tassel.

6) Wrap gimp or narrow braid over the binding. Turn under end of gimp; hand-stitch. Stitch several times straight through tassel to secure. Trim tassel end evenly.

How to Make Fringe End Caps

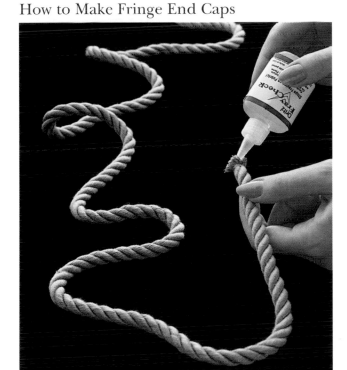

1) Bind cord with heavy thread ¼" (6 mm) from end. Apply liquid fray preventer to cord end. Allow to dry.

2) Wrap fringe twice around cord end, covering binding. Turn under heading; hand-stitch. Stitch several times straight through end cap to secure.

Index

References for contributors' products:

A. Svensson & Company, pp. 16, 17

Bandex Home Decorating
Corporation, p. 96 (pleater tape)

Bentley Brothers, p. 16

Conso Products Company, pp. 57,
108-109, 110, 117, 123

Dritz Corporation, pp. 9, 16, 17, 37,
80, 81, 95, 122

Gene Smiley Showroom, pp. 102
(tassels), 118-119

Graber Industries, Inc., pp. 16, 17,
72 (shade undertreatment), 78-79
(rod), 102-103, 114-115 (shade
undertreatment)

Hirshfields Design Studio, pp. 108-109
(tassels)

Kirsh Division, Cooper Industries, Inc.,
pp. 11, 16, 17, 88-89, 94 (holdbacks)

Murta Industries, U.S.A., pp. 94, 95, 96

Swavelle/Mill Creek Textiles, pp. 81
(lining), 110 (piping)

Waverly, Division of F. Schumacher &
Company, cover, pp. 2-3, 6, 7, 13, 14,
15, 22-23, 24 and 25 (band fabric), 42-
43, 44, 46, 47, 49, 50-51, 52, 57, 78-79,
88-89 (tabs), 94 (sheers), 95, 108-109,
114-115 (trim), 118-119, 123

Cowles Creative Publishing, Inc.
offers a variety of how-to books. For
information write:
  Cowles Creative Publishing
   Subscriber Books
  5900 Green Oak Drive
  Minnetonka, MN 55343